PICTURE HISTORY OF
AMERICAN PASSENGER SHIPS

William H. Miller, Jr.

DOVER PUBLICATIONS, INC.
Mineola, New York

This book is dedicated to
Historic Hoboken
the perfect spot for watching the
Great Ocean Liners

&

Copyright

Copyright © 2001 by William H. Miller, Jr.
All rights reserved under Pan American and International Copyright
Conventions

Published in Canada by General Publishing Company, Ltd., 30 Lesmill
Road, Don Mills, Toronto, Ontario

Bibliographical Note

Picture History of American Passenger Ships is a new work, first published by
Dover Publications, Inc., in 2001.

Library of Congress Cataloging-in-Publication Data

Miller, William H., 1948–
    Picture history of American passenger ships / William H. Miller, Jr.
       p. cm.
    Includes bibliographical references and index.
    ISBN 0-486-40967-8 (pbk.)
     1. Passenger ships—United States—Pictorial works. I. Title
VM381 .M449823 2001
387.5'42'0973—dc21

                         00-052379
                         CIP

Book design by Carol Belanger Grafton

Manufactured in the United States of America
Dover Publications, Inc., 31 East 2nd Street, Mineola, N.Y. 11501

Preface

I met Bill Miller, appropriately enough, on the deck of a ship. It was love at first sight: the meeting of two "ship people." For me, it was like reconnecting with a childhood teacher whom I hadn't seen in years; a mentor whose books had taught me of the French Line, the *Canberra*, the "old" *Rotterdam*. We had never met, but we knew each other well. I, the shipboard editor of the daily newspaper aboard the *Crystal Symphony*; Bill, a "Crystal Cruises Favorite" lecturer, on board as he often was to spin a yarn (or two or three) about those luxury liners of the past.

Often during that cruise, and others, we would find each other on deck—both having raced up separately to look at the facade of a passing liner.

"That used to be the old . . ." and we would laugh and begin that favorite game of ship lovers: guess the ship. Bill was never wrong, and could recite the provenance of passing vessels on the horizon or tied-up in Piraeus (does anyone buy more old ships than the Greeks?) like some master sommelier holding forth about a rare vintage.

I had always known that some day, somehow, I would "go to sea." As a boy growing up in land-locked Richmond, Virginia, I would gaze longingly from our pool, where in usual precision, I was guiding a flotilla of plastic models, or at the cinder-blocked hull of our 25-foot cabin cruiser "docked" next to the patio. Any day now, the tarpaulins of plastic would give way to the sticky preparation of hull varnish. Soon, my Pop would back up the trailer and pull this "Gilligan's Island"-like boat to its rightful home: the Chesapeake Bay, a short two-hour drive away. My mother would make sandwiches, cover my blond nose with sun block, and warn us (successfully) to "clean the fish" before we came home.

I hated fishing, and still do. But, on the way to my father's favorite spot—above the wreck of an old freighter (a thought that always terrified and excited me)—Pop and I would pass by the Newport News shipyard. Here was the catch for me, like a huge whale in its tank—confined but still crowd-pleasing—the SS *United States*, the greatest liner ever built in America. What a beauty!

This was in the days (not so long ago) before guests going on board a passenger ship had to swipe magnetic strips through computers or submit to the indelicate necessities of metal detectors. In those "good old days" of the late 1960s and early '70s, the only thing the *United States'* keepers were afraid of was someone jumping on board to make off with a memento! Of course, when the great ship was built, so secret was the design of her hull (a speed of forty-plus knots made her a potentially formidable troopship during those Cold War climes) that the Revell model I played with in my pool was flat below the water-line!

Once—a memory preserved in fading Polaroids—we actually pulled alongside the liner, and I reached my ten-year-old hand to touch the peeling red paint along her port side. That same day the carrier *John F. Kennedy* was tied up alongside as well, and I remember waving and shouting to the sailors on board. For a kid into ships it was like a pilgrimage to St. Peter's Basilica for Roman Catholics. I did the best I could to peer at her gracefully curving physique of the "Big U" hiding beneath the salty waters of her quay. What was the secret of her speed!

I remember telling that story to Bill Miller, and his eyes lit up.

Of course, as one of the world's greatest authorities on the behemoth designed by William Francis Gibbs, Bill was always in search of a new story, a fresh perspective on this holder of the Blue Riband. Right then and there he asked me to write the preface for his next book: one on the subject about which far too little has been written—American passenger vessels.

Now, finally, such a book is here. Undoubtedly, Bill Miller has given us yet another "must have" in the reference library of ships.

As I write this, in port in Honolulu harbor—a stopoff on the *Crystal Symphony*'s annual world cruise—the very last American-flagged liner, the *Independence*, is tied up across from us. Even with the designer-gone-mad color scheme she has been subjected to, she is still every inch a lady.

For those of us who long for such sights, who rush to the rail as the wreck of the *America* is sighted off the Canaries, who talk their way on board the old (and still so-named) *Monterey* while docked in Kusadasi, and who love nothing better than curling up with a book whose ballast is photos and facts about liners, this is a treasure for you. As with all of Bill's books, here in your hands is the definitive work on American passenger vessels.

Bon Voyage!

DAVID PERRY
Aboard *Crystal Symphony*
January 1999

Acknowledgements

A great many people have been extraordinarily generous in helping me create this book. They have shared their knowledge, their collections—those cherished brochures, sailing schedules, and booklets—and, most of all, their recollections and insights. But most of all they have extended their prized photos, black-and-white reproductions that perhaps document these ships better than anything else. I also deeply appreciate their continued encouragement and patience, for there are so often mountains to climb and overcome, and those unavoidable delays. I understand always their prime concern: Are the pictures safe and soon to be returned?

Ernest Arroyo is not only a prince among men and world-class nautical collector and historian, but a true hero. He saved the priceless photo collection of the late Frank Cronican, himself a giant in the annals of American marine history as well as being a flawless ship modelmaker. Drawers of photos might have ended in a trash bin. Many of Cronican's photos now see the light of day thanks to Arroyo's intervention and incredible generosity. These photos have legally passed to another dear and most sharing friend, Richard Faber, surely one of the world's greatest ocean liner collectors and memorabilia dealers.

I must give great thanks as well to three icons of ocean liner history: Frank Braynard, John Gillespie, and Everett Viez. These men amassed superb collections of pictures without which we would not have so many passenger ship books. I would also like to thank Frank Duffy, who graciously shared the vast photo files of the Moran Towing & Transportation Company, a firm that handled so many of the ships included in these pages.

Special thanks to two other fine men, author-anthropologist Jack Weatherford and writer David Perry, both friends from many voyages aboard Crystal Cruises.

Further appreciation goes to Tom Cangialosi, Erhard Koehler, James L. Shaw, and Stephen L. Tacey.

Firms, some of which are, alas, are no more, which assisted include the American President Lines, Carnival Cruise Lines, Flying Camera Inc, Grace Line, Matson Lines, Moore-McCormack Lines, Moran Towing & Transportation Company, Norshipco, United States Lines, and the World City Corporation. I am also particularly grateful to Dover Publications for taking on this project and to my dear friends Tom Cassidy and Abe Michaelson. Without each of them, there would not be such books.

Introduction

On a November afternoon in 1998 ocean liner aficionados and historians joined the officials of Carnival Cruise Lines, the biggest passenger ship operator of all time, for a reception on board their newest cruiseship to date, the 70,200-ton *Paradise*. The huge, all-white liner, the latest in a long line of modern-day floating hotels, was berthed for the occasion in the south slip of Pier 88, at the foot of West 48th Street, along Manhattan's Hudson River waterfront. In a matter of days the 860-foot-long vessel would move on to her home base at Miami, sailing on weekly cruises to the sunny waters of the Caribbean. The week-long visit to Manhattan was part of the inaugurals for the $350 million ship. The last unit of an eight-ship series—in fact, the greatest passenger liner of its kind in history—she was unique in several other ways as well. She was the very first totally smoke-free vessel for the booming American cruise industry. She used the advanced Azipod propulsion system, which made her one of the most operationally efficient ships yet built. Her overall decor was special, too: It was a celebration of the great liners of the past, notably the legendary ships that plied the North Atlantic route to and from Europe. And while *Paradise* is home to the Queen Mary Lounge and the Cafe Ile de France, her decoration celebrated in many ways the great age of American passenger ships. Carnival is, after all, based in Miami, while using foreign flags of convenience for its ever-expanding fleet. They even use red, white, and blue on their raked, fin-topped smokestacks. Notably, on board the 2,600-passenger *Paradise* there were bars named for the liners *United States* and *America*, and a library that honors the illustrious Blue Riband, the prized trophy once given for the fastest passage on the Atlantic. The 53,300-ton *United States* was the last luxury liner to have the honor. She was the fastest merchant ship afloat starting with her 1952 maiden voyage. The ceremony on board the *Paradise* was in honor of that record and, in fact, a salute not only to that great ship, but generally to all American passenger vessels.

The Blue Riband record and the accompanying trophy that went with it were passed on to the little catamaran-ferry *Hoverspeed Great Britain* in the summer of 1990. The *United States*, then still laid up at a Norfolk, Virginia, pier and in deepening decay, had not sailed in twenty-one years. Even her once mighty owners, the United States Lines, were out of business, bankrupted in 1986 by economic miscalculations and shifts in the balance of the fiercely competitive U.S.-flag container-cargo business. The Riband and even the trophy itself went to the *Hoverspeed*'s owners, Sea Containers Ltd, who keep it in their London headquarters. But with the *Paradise* Carnival restored something of the glory that was once held by the *United States* and other Yankee passenger ships. While having a copy of the Blue Riband trophy made for the library on board the *Paradise*, they ordered a second duplicate, which was cere-

moniously presented to maritime author-historian Frank Braynard, the founder and curator of the United States Merchant Marine Museum at Kings Point, New York. The original trophy had been there, standing in glass-encased, spotlighted splendor, until moved to Sea Containers House, located on the banks of the River Thames in the heart of London. (In fact, just months before I attended this event, in June 1998, another fast ferry, the Argentine-owned *Catalonia*, made a special voyage from New York to Tarifa, Spain, and surpassed even the *Hoverspeed Great Britain*'s record. The Mediterranean-based, passenger-and-auto-carrying *Catalonia* crossed at a record of 38.8 knots, compared to the 35.5 knots of the *United States* forty-six years before and to the slightly higher rate of the *Hoverspeed*.)

The *United States* herself, still caught in her seemingly unending limbo of idleness and neglect (although at a Philadelphia pier by 1998), is still a compelling presence. Rumors of her reactivation—probably not as a refitted cruiseship but as a moored hotel and/or convention center—are followed closely by many ship historians. In part she inspired this book. So did the 1932-built former *Monterey*, which had sailed as the Greek-owned cruise ship *Britanis* until the mid-1990s. Although her actual steaming days had passed, she was still afloat in 1998, a testament to American passenger ship construction and overall design. She still had her original steam turbines, for example. In addition, a number of other former U.S.-flag passenger ships are still traveling about—the former *Santa Rosa*, *Argentina*, *Brasil*, and a subsequent *Monterey* (this one built in 1952). Each of them appears in this book.

I chose the *Leviathan* as my starting point. Unlike the Europeans, namely the British and the Germans before the First World War, Americans had not had a superliner of their own (even though New York was the great western terminus of the Atlantic trade). The *Leviathan* had come to U.S. service indirectly, however, having been the German *Vaterland* in her first life. After the war, and while falling short of the supership class, the Americans built many significant ships: the advanced *Malolo* of 1927, the enduring *Monterey* and her two sisters of 1932, and the steamlined *Panama* class of 1939. The P2-Class troopships were the largest purposely built transports of the 1940s, while the *Independence* of 1951 was the first fully air conditioned luxury liner. The giant *United States* was, of course, notable in many ways and was by far the most advanced ship of her time. Indeed, the American liners make a very interesting fleet. Hopefully, this book of photographs will add to their record.

BILL MILLER
Secaucus, New Jersey
December 1998

Picture Credits

Cronican-Arroyo Collection: pages 2(top), 3, 4, 5, 6, 7, 9, 10, 11, 12, 13(top), 14, 15, 17, 18, 19(top), 20(top), 22(top), 24, 25(bottom), 26, 28(top), 32, 33, 34(top), 35, 37, 40(top), 42, 43, 44(bottom), 45, 46(bottom), 48, 49(top), 50(top), 51, 52, 53(middle & bottom), 54, 55(top & bottom left), 56, 57, 58, 59(top & middle), 61, 62, 63(bottom), 66, 67(top), 68(top), 70, 71(bottom), 73(top), 74, 75(bottom), 83(bottom), 85(top), 90(top & bottom right), 91(bottom), 92, 93(top), 94(bottom), 95, 96(top & bottom), 97, 100, 101(top), 102, 103(bottom), 104, 105, 106, 109(bottom), 111, 112

Frank O. Braynard Collection: pages 2(bottom), 49(bottom), 75(top), 79(bottom), 83(top), 84, 85(bottom), 86, 87(top), 88(top), 93(bottom), 94(top), 96(middle), 101(bottom)

Ernest Arroyo Collection: pages 19(bottom), 47, 64(top), 71(top), 78, 79(top), 80, 81, 83(bottom)

Richard Faber Collection: pages 20(bottom), 21, 22(bottom), 46(top), 55(bottom right), 73(bottom), 103(top), 110(top)

Everett Viez Collection: pages 27, 29, 30, 34(bottom), 38

Gillespie-Faber Collection: pages 36, 39, 40(bottom), 53(top)

United States Lines: pages 44(top), 63(top), 64(bottom), 65, 67(bottom), 90(bottom left), 91(top), 107

Moran Towing & Transportation Company: pages 50(bottom), 76(top)

Flying Camera, Inc.: pages 88(bottom), 98, 99(top), 110(bottom), 114

Hamburg America Line: page 13(bottom); Moore-McCormack Lines: page 28(bottom); James L. Shaw Collection: page 59(bottom); Steven L. Tacey: page 68(bottom); Farrell Lines: page 72(bottom); Alcoa Steamship Company: page 76(bottom); Gordon Turner Collection: page 82; Sea-Land Service: page 87(bottom); American Hawaii Cruises: page 99(bottom); Norshipco: page 108(top); Tom Cangialosi: page 108(bottom); Matson Lines: page 109(top); John Gillespie Collection: page 113; Andy Newman/Carnival Cruise Lines: page 115(top); World City Corporation: page 115(bottom)

Contents

CHAPTER 1
America's First Superliner: *Leviathan* / 1

CHAPTER 2
Acquisitions, Seizures, and Other Prizes of War / 8

CHAPTER 3
Standard Classes / 16

CHAPTER 4
The Late Twenties: Big New Liners / 23

CHAPTER 5
Small Ships of the Prewar Era / 31

CHAPTER 6
Expansion: Building Up the Fleet / 41

CHAPTER 7
New National Flagship: *America* / 60

CHAPTER 8
"Combo" Ships: Passengers and Cargo / 69

CHAPTER 9
Serving the Military During and After World War II / 77

CHAPTER 10
Modern American Luxury at Sea / 89

Bibliography / 116

Index of Ships in Illustrations / 117

CHAPTER 1

America's First Superliner: *Leviathan*

"She was our great national treasure of a ship," according to Frank O. Braynard, author of a monumental five-volume series about the *Leviathan*, but she was launched in Hamburg, Germany, early in 1914 as the *Vaterland*. She was in regular transatlantic service for only a few months before the Kaiser declared war on France, on August 3, 1914. In a major miscalculation by the German naval command, the *Vaterland* was berthed in the U.S., at Hoboken, New Jersey, when the war began. Unable to return across the Atlantic to Germany, she sat for almost three years before being seized by the U.S., which had entered the war on April 6, 1917.

The great ship eventually proved to be of significant value to the Americans. "She had size, speed, and luxury," said Braynard. "Everyone knew her from the First World War, when, as the trooper USS *Leviathan*, she established a heroic record. She carried the greatest number of troops, those famous 'doughboys,' to Europe, then later returned them to gala welomes in New York Harbor. One of her younger crew members was a quartermaster named Humphrey Bogart. After the war the *Leviathan* was extremely popular. She was perfect as America's first superliner, a true competitor to the other big liners of the day, such as the *Mauretania*, *Aquitania*, *Berengaria*, *Majestic*, and *Olympic*. In the 1920s her name was everywhere—newspapers, magazines, and posters. She was a huge ship, over 500,000 tons, dwarfing the tiny tugboats alongside. She did have structural weaknesses, however, including two cracks that occurred."

After the war the *Leviathan* was the great hope of the U.S. government, which claimed her as a war prize, and of the United States Lines, her operators. The new age of tourism brought on by postwar prosperity seemed made for the magnificent ship. "The 1920s was the decade that many Americans discovered Europe as a vacation destination," said author-historian Jack Weatherford. "Europe was cheap, and the romance of it was heightened not only by stories from World War soldiers but also by the writings of F. Scott Fitzgerald, Ernest Hemingway, and others. It was the place to have a good time, and that good time was said to begin at the New York City piers." For all those who wanted to escape Prohibition and the insularity of life in many areas of the U.S., a voyage to Europe was the way to go.

Despite increased transatlantic travel, the high hopes for the *Leviathan* were never fully realized. She lost millions of dollars; even at her peak, in the mid-1920s, she attracted only about 50 percent of her passenger capacity for transatlantic voyages. Sailing under the U.S. flag proved to be a disadvantage. Prohibition extended to American ships, as did the U.S. reputation for inferior cuisine and service. In contrast, the French Line, the Cunard Line, and other foreign-flag companies touted their European ambience. Another problem was that the *Leviathan* did not have a proper running-mate to fill out the round-trip schedule. At best, she was paired with the smaller *George Washington* and *America*. Finally, the *Leviathan* was expensive to run and maintain. Costs were almost always higher for American ships than for those of European lines.

The Depression made things even worse. In the early 1930s she was idle more often than she sailed, and soon she was permanently moored at the Second Street pier in Hoboken. Meanwhile, a new generation of superliners such as the French *Normandie* and the Cunarder *Queen Mary* sailed grandly past the *Leviathan* as the rust on her superstructure thickened and as her lounges and cabins grew colder and mustier. Finally, on a bleak day in January 1938 she set off for Scotland and the shipbreakers.

Despite her problems, the great ship, surely one of the most famous floating palaces of the time, left a deep impression on many people. "Because of the *Leviathan*, I started saving objects from ocean liners," said Frank Braynard, who went on to amass one of the largest maritime collections in the world. "It was 1923, and I was seven years old. That same year I did a sketch of the *Leviathan*. I spelled the ship's name correctly, but misspelled my own last name."

LEVIATHAN. In one of the great miscalculations made during World War I, the Germans left their largest and finest liner, the *Vaterland*, in U.S. waters. On the very day that the Kaiser's generals began warfare the ship was at her Hoboken, New Jersey, berth. She remained there for the next three years—silent, rusting, caught in a strange limbo. Actually, early in the war, she was used as a setting for fund-raising events by the German-American community. The monies were then sent to support the Kaiser's war effort. But as the United States became more seriously involved in the war, especially after the tragic sinking of the Cunard Line's *Lusitania* in May 1915, the giant *Vaterland* became "restricted property." She was officially seized in April 1917 and became the USS *Leviathan*, the largest troopship in Allied service. She is seen here *(left)* making a triumphant arrival in New York's Upper Bay with returning servicemen on board. The date is December 1918. [Built by Blohm & Voss Shipbuilders, Hamburg, Germany, 1914. 54,282 gross tons; 950 feet long; 100 feet wide; 35-foot draft. Steam turbines, quadruple screw. Service speed 23 knots. 3,391 passengers as *Leviathan* (970 first class, 542 second class, 944 third class, 935 fourth class).]

After the war ended, the *Leviathan* sat at her Hoboken pier once again. Officials in Washington debated her future and finally decided to refit the ship for the newly formed United States Lines, making her flagship of the entire American merchant marine. She was sent to the huge Newport News Shipbuilding & Drydock Company yard in Virginia in 1921 to begin a two-year restoration. Thousands of workers were employed on the project. Electrical wiring had to be replaced, piping redone, the engines restored, and the passenger quarters brought up to higher standards. Because loyalist German crew members had sabotaged some of her machinery and later refused to supply proper plans for the ship, the brilliant naval architect William Francis Gibbs had to begin the conversion of the ship as if she was brand new. In July 1923 she steamed up the Hudson River *(above)*, back from her first postwar commercial journey. The sixty-story Woolworth Building is on the right, the forty-seven-story Singer Tower on the far left.

An opulent Ritz-Carlton Grill *(left)*, adjunct to the restaurant in first class, was a feature of some German liners before the First World War. The *Vaterland*'s popular grill was carried over to the *Leviathan*. United States Lines' publicity boasted, "True, it is unusual to have thick, rich, fresh cream at every meal . . . meats from blue-ribbon stock . . . pheasant, grouse and quail under glass . . . strawberries and melons when New York is bending to a snowstorm . . . caviar that is not just caviar, but Malossal . . . and coffee prepared and served as only those in America can prepare and serve it. But the *Leviathan* is an extraordinary ship, and her chef catered for an emperor!" One brochure summarized the ship's service: "The stamp of an international traveler is the utterance: 'I crossed on the *Leviathan*.'"

An addition to the *Leviathan* during her postwar refit was the contemporary-styled nightclub, the Club Leviathan *(right)*. "You have listened to the 'talkies,' the latest child of science, far out in the Atlantic," read one lavish booklet on the ship, "and then taken a last stroll around the promenade deck before entering the Club Leviathan. An architectural masterpiece of modernistic spirit, yet possessing a little of Egypt in the days of the pharaohs, Club Leviathan is incense to those who seek the novel and the new. You enter it over a carpet of gold ornamented with a jet-black note . . . lovely couples are dancing in a color web of changing lights . . . tall embrasures fling shafts of fire skyward . . . a Ben Bernie orchestra is breathing vivacity into jazz . . . parties are sipping and supping the hours away in crescent-shaped enclosures, cushioned in scarlet and agleam with the soft play of light on rich lacquers."

This first-class stateroom *(left)* on board the *Leviathan* was furnished with twin beds, a long sofa, a desk and cupboard area, and even a fireplace.

The imposing entrance to the ship's Grand Salon *(above)* was one of the most opulent areas in first class.

The *Leviathan* encounters some stormy North Atlantic weather with great waves slapping over her foredeck *(opposite, top)*. The United States Lines took great effort to reassure their passengers about safety, remembering that the *Titanic* had sunk little more than a decade before, on April 15, 1912. Literature about the *Leviathan* read, "Rarely does one speak of safety devices on the *Leviathan*—for she is a symbol of safety. There's 'Metal Mike'—as mariners call it—a device used in the pilot house to keep the ship on her course more accurately than human hand or mind can. And the fathometer, which automatically registers the depth of water under the *Leviathan's* keel. A lighted switchboard on the bridge which shows the condition of every bulkhead door opened or closed, and which controls any or all merely by the touch of a finger. Then there's the great 'night eye,' a high-intensity searchlight of 450,000 candle-power, which leads you through the darkened seas."

For all her size and grandeur, the *Leviathan* was never a highly successful liner. She lost more and more money as the Depression set in, finally being laid up in 1932. Then, rather oddly, she was reactivated in the spring of 1934, but for only four more Atlantic voyages. She is seen *(opposite, bottom)* at the Boston Navy Yard on May 28, 1934, being repainted for her short-lived return to service.

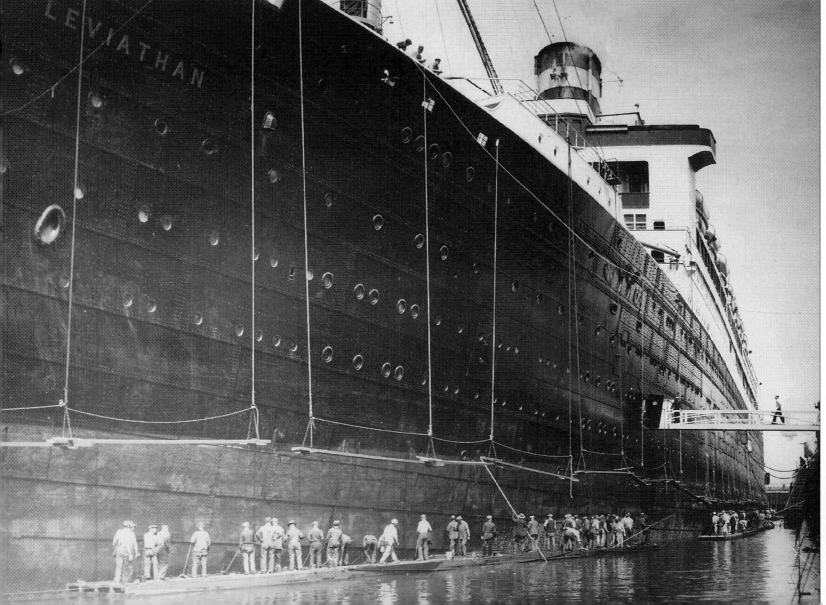

Laid up and fading, the *Leviathan* sat on the south side of New York City's Pier 59, at the foot of West 19th Street, before being towed across the Hudson to Hoboken. There were rumors that she might be revived for further service, but nothing came to pass. Over the next two years she fell into deepening decay. This view from her port bridge (*left*) shows the weather-beaten condition of her massive three funnels, the upper decks, and some of her lifeboats. The date is October 5, 1937.

With her masts and funnels specially shortened to clear the Firth of Forth Bridge in Scotland, the *Leviathan* (*opposite, top*) raised steam and left Hoboken on January 25, 1938. It was her last voyage, bound for the scrapyard at Rosyth.

On February 15 the former pride of the German and then the American merchant navies arrived in Scotland (*opposite, bottom*) for breaking up. In a matter of months she was gone completely.

The former first-class dining room (*right*) was stripped and desolate, a haunting reminder of more glorious, fun-filled days on the Atlantic. Queen Marie of Rumania and Gloria Swanson, among other notables, had once dined here.

CHAPTER 2

Acquisitions, Seizures, and Other Prizes of War

In the years before the First World War the U.S. Merchant Marine was sinking into deep stagnation. The Americans had no big ocean liners—in fact, no passenger ships of note in any size—and no plans for any. British and German companies carried about 75 percent of the traffic in and out of New York Harbor, and there was little U.S. interest in competing on the popular transatlantic run. All this changed when the U.S. entered World War I on the side of the Allies. In order to get men and materiel to Europe, the military needed ships. The High Command in Washington ordered that a massive shipbuilding program go into high gear immediately. Millions of tons in new shipping were launched as the government's construction program continued after the Armistice was signed late in 1918.

Fortunately, more immediate needs could be met by German-flag vessels abandoned in 1914 at the Hoboken piers used by the Hamburg America Line and North German Lloyd. These vessels, seized by the U.S., in total had greater tonnage and value than the entire American merchant fleet that had existed in 1914. The greatest prize, of course, was the *Vaterland*, quickly converted into the *Leviathan*. Another was *Kronprinz Wilhelm*, which became the U.S. Navy trooper *Von Steuben*. Both ships were among the largest, fastest, and most luxurious ocean liners of the day. Amazingly, three of these five fell into American hands. The other two captives in this class, the *Kaiser Wilhelm II* and the *Kronprinzessin Cecile*, were also converted into troopships, renamed USS *Monticello* and USS *Mount Vernon*, respectively. Plans were made to restore these two behemoths to passenger service after the war, but nothing came to pass. Both ships sat in layup for over twenty years before going to the shipbreakers in 1940. Though another war had begun, they were too old to be of any use to the Allies.

Among other German ships seized by the U.S. and converted for use by the American military were the *Amerika* (renamed *America*), the *President Grant*, and the *George Washington*. The ships had been given these names at launch to attract emigrants leaving Germany, many of whom believed that sailing on ships with American-sounding names would give them a better chance of successful entry at Ellis Island. For commercial passenger service the *President Grant* was renamed the *Republic*, while the other two ships kept their names. All three were recalled to service in World War II, with the *America* being renamed the *Edmund B. Alexander*. Other ships in this group were either interned in ports outside the U.S. or came into American hands as war reparations.

MOUNT VERNON. When completed in the summer of 1907, North German Lloyd's *Kronprinzessin Cecilie* joined Germany's other four-stackers—the *Kaiser Wilhelm der Grosse* (1897), the *Deutschland* (1900), the *Kronprinz Wilhelm* (1901), and the *Kaiser Wilhelm II* (1903). They were among the fastest and finest Atlantic liners of their day. All except the *Deutschland* would be lost to the Germans during the First World War. The *Kronprinzessin Cecilie* was off the American East Coast on July 29, 1914, when word was received that war in Europe was imminent. Her position was especially troublesome. She was carrying not only German passengers, but also a prized cargo of $10 million in gold bars and $1 million in silver bound for the Kaiser's banks. Her master soon realized that a safe eastbound passage was improbable; capture by the British would be likely. Instead, a clever scheme was devised. The ship's radio was silenced, and she sailed only at night, without any lights. She reversed course for U.S. waters, with her funnels repainted in White Star Line colors so that she could be mistaken for the far larger, British-flag *Olympic,* sister to the *Titanic.* Some of her passengers were angry, others excited by the mysterious maneuvers. A third group offered to buy the ship so that they could hoist the American flag and openly sail for a neutral port.

The German liner soon anchored in the placid waters of Bar Harbor, Maine. At first the disguise worked. Word spread locally that the "Olympic" was in the harbor. But when that news reached New York, it was reported that White Star's *Olympic* was, in fact, at her West Side berth. The German liner, along with her valuable cargo, was soon interned by American authorities. The *Cecilie* was moved to Boston and laid up there for nearly three years. In April 1917 she was transferred to the U.S. Navy and renamed USS *Mount Vernon* **(above).** Refitted as a troopship, she served well, making many transatlantic voyages before being laid up in 1919. There were plans to refit her as a commercial liner for United States Lines, perhaps even converting her engines to diesel power, but these never came to pass. Instead, she was laid up in Chesapeake Bay for nearly twenty years. In 1940 she was offered to the British government for further use as a troopship, but they declined in view of her age. That same year she was sold to scrappers at Baltimore and quickly broken up. [Built by Vulkan Shipyards, Stettin, German, 1906. 19,360 gross tons; 707 feet long; 72 feet wide. Steam quadruple-expansion engines, twin screw. Service speed 23 knots. 1,970 passengers as built (558 first class, 338 second class, 1,074 steerage).]

GEORGE WASHINGTON. Another German liner caught at her Hoboken pier in August 1914 was the *George Washington* of North German Lloyd. She sat idle until April 1917, when she became the Navy troopship USS *George Washington*, or, as she was known, the "Big George." She had a loyal following and was known as a durable ship. In 1919 she was selected to carry President Woodrow Wilson and his party to the Peace Conference at Versailles. They departed in March and returned on the same ship that August. She was refitted for commercial service for the United States Lines, and by 1921 she was sailing the North Atlantic on a regular run that included calls at New York, Southampton, Cherbourg, and Bremerhaven. In 1925 the *Washington* was refitted in the large graving dock at the Boston Naval Shipyard (*opposite*), then continued in transatlantic service until 1931, when she was laid up on the Patuxent River in Maryland. In 1940 she was reactivated for use as a troop transport, soon to be leased to the hard-pressed British, who renamed her *Catlin*. The old ship's machinery was troublesome, however, and she was soon returned to the U.S. Navy and reverted to her original name. She barely managed a sluggish eleven knots, and in 1942–43 she was rebuilt with new boilers and a single stack. After the war, in March 1947, she was badly damaged by fire at her New York berth. She was moved to Baltimore and laid up, only to be totally destroyed there, on January 17, 1951, when a dock fire spread to the former liner. She was soon scrapped. [Built by Vulkan Shipyards, Stettin, Germany, 1909. 25,570 gross tons; 723 feet long; 72 feet wide. Steam quadruple-expansion engines, twin screw. Service speed 18.5 knots. 2,679 passengers as built (568 first class, 433 second class, 452 third class, 1,226 steerage).]

AMERICA (1905). Still another German liner caught in U.S. waters as the First War started was Hamburg-America Line's *Amerika*. When completed in October 1905 (and for about a year afterward), she was the largest ocean liner afloat. Interned at Boston in August 1914, she was not reactivated until April 1917, when she became the Navy trooper USS *America*. She sank at her berth in New York harbor while taking on coal on October 15, 1918. Six were killed in the accident. Raised that December, she was repaired, and resumed trooping. In 1921 she began sailing on the North Atlantic for the United States Lines. The great ship was nearly lost to fire when being overhauled at the Newport News shipyard in Virginia in March 1926. She is seen (*above*) arriving in New York on January 26, 1929. Laid up owing to the Depression in 1931, she sat in Chesapeake Bay until refitted in 1940–41 as the modernized troopship USS *Edmund B. Alexander*. She was rebuilt once again, in 1942, and was fitted with a single stack. Laid up again in 1949, she sat in the Hudson River Reserve Fleet near Bear Mountain, New York, until sold to scrappers at Baltimore in 1958. [Built by Harland & Wolff Limited, Belfast, Northern Ireland, 1905. 22,225 gross tons; 700 feet long; 74 feet wide. Steam quadruple-expansion engines, twin screw. Service speed 17.5 knots. 2,662 passengers as built (420 first class, 252 second class, 223 third class, 1,765 steerage).]

IDLE QUARTET. Aerial view *(top)* of four ex-German liners in layup, Patuxent River, off Chesapeake Bay, 1939. From left to right, they are the *Monticello*, ex-*Kaiser Wilhelm II*; the *Mount Vernon*, ex-*Kronprinzessin Cecilie*; the *America*, ex-*Amerika*; and the *George Washington*. That December it was announced by the Federal Maritime Commission that the aged quartet would be sold for scrap. In fact, the first two were offered to the British and then scrapped, but both the *America* and the *George Washington* were later refitted for duties in the Second World War.

An interesting collection of rusting smokestacks *(bottom)*: a view from the *George Washington*, laid up in Chesapeake Bay, dated June 28, 1934, showing the *Monticello* at the far end, the *Mount Vernon*, and then closest, one stack of the *America*.

REPUBLIC. Another former German was the *President Grant* of the Hamburg-America Line. Laid down as the *Servian* for British owners, she was bought by the Germans while still under construction in 1906 and was scheduled to be renamed *Boston*. Instead, she was completed as the six-masted *President Grant*, a large passenger-cargo liner capable of carrying as many as 3,830 passengers. Interned at Hoboken in August 1914, she returned to service in 1917 as a U.S. Navy transport. Rebuilt for commercial passenger service for the United States Lines in 1923–24, she was renamed *Republic* for North Atlantic sailings. She is shown *(above)*, on June 25, 1930, departing from the Second Street pier in Hoboken with 302 Gold Star Mothers on board, en route to visit the graves of their sons in France. In 1931 the *Republic* was transferred to the U.S. Army and used as a peacetime troopship. She saw further duties in the Second World War and later spent part of 1945 as a hospital ship. She was scrapped in 1952. [Built by Harland & Wolff Limited, Belfast, Northern Ireland, 1907. 18,168 gross tons; 616 feet long; 68 feet wide. Steam quadruple-expansion engines, twin screw. Service speed 14.5 knots. 3,830 passengers as built (326 first class, 152 second class, 1,004 third class, 2,348 steerage).

RELIANCE. Almost all of the German passenger ship fleet was lost or confiscated by the end of World War I. Two intended liners for the Hamburg-America Line were the near-sisters *William O'Swald* and *Johann Heinrich Burchard*, which were still under construction when the conflict began in August 1914. But under a wartime sale agreement and then as part of postwar reparations, they went to the Dutch. The Royal Holland Lloyd of Amsterdam renamed them the *Brabantia* and the *Limburgia*, respectively. They sailed between Amsterdam and the east coast of South America. Amidst technical problems and general lack of profits, however, they were sold in 1922 to the New York-based United American Lines, raised the American colors, and became the *Resolute* and the *Reliance (below)*, respectively. Ironically, they were used on their intended service between New York and Hamburg, and in conjunction with their original Hamburg-America owners. A year later, in 1923, they were among the first liners to use a flag of convenience, Panama, to avoid the restrictions of the U.S. Prohibition era. In 1926 they were sold outright to Hamburg-America. They continued on the Atlantic route and subsequently established fine reputations as all-one-class cruise ships. The *Resolute* was sold to the Italian government in 1935 for use as a troopship in Mussolini's African campaigns as the *Lombardia*. She was sunk at Naples in 1943, and her wreck was scrapped three years later. The *Reliance* burned in Hamburg harbor in August 1938, and her wreckage was broken up for the Nazi war effort in 1941. [Built by J. C. Tecklenborg shipyard, Geestemunde, Germany, 1920. 19,582 gross tons; 615 feet long; 71 feet wide. Triple-expansion engines and one steam turbine, triple screw. Service speed 16 knots. 1,010 passengers (290 first class, 320 second class, 400 third class).]

U. S. GRANT. Hamburg-America's *Kaiser Wilhelm II* was used on several runs before World War I: Hamburg to the east coast of South America, to the West Indies, and occasionally on the North Atlantic to New York. She was seized in the war and became the troop transport *Madawaska*, then the *General Ulysses S. Grant*, and finally in 1922 the *U. S. Grant (top)*. She sailed for the U.S. Army in peacetime service, then did further trooping in the Second World War. She was laid up at Seattle in 1946 before being scrapped a year later. [Built by Vulkan Shipyard, Stettin, Germany, 1907. 9,410 gross tons; 490 feet long; 55 feet wide. Quadruple-expansion engines, twin screw. Service speed 15 knots. 1,025 passengers as built (326 first class, 44 second class, 655 third class).]

CITY OF HONOLULU. The *Kiautschou* was one of eleven sisters and near-sisters that belonged to the Hamburg-America Line as well as North German Lloyd. She ran between Bremerhaven and New York as well as on crossings to and from the Mediterranean and on long-distance voyages from Bremerhaven to Australia via the Suez Canal. She was interned at Manila in August 1914, then reactivated in 1917 for American-flag service as the transport USS *Princess Matoika*. Afterward, in 1919, she was refitted for commercial service for the United States Shipping Board, then the United States Mail Steamship Company, and finally the United States Lines. She sailed from New York to Naples and Genoa, to Bremen and to Danzig. In 1922 she was rechristened *President Arthur*, then sold three years later to the newly formed American Palestine Line for New York–Haifa service. They planned to rename her *White Palace*, but this project never developed and instead she was resold, first to New York owners, then to the Los Angeles Steamship Company for Hawaiian islands cruise service. Renamed *City of Honolulu*, she was fitted out with quarters for 445 first-class and a mere 50 third-class passengers. Unfortunately, she burned at Honolulu on May 25, 1930, and was declared a complete loss. She was then laid up at Los Angeles *(middle)*. The end came in August 1933, when she was sold to Japanese shipbreakers and brought to Osaka for demolition. [Built by the Vulkan Shipyard, Stettin, Germany, 1900. 10,911 gross tons; 540 feet long; 60 feet wide. Steam quadruple-expansion engines, twin screw. Service speed 15.5 knots. 495 passsengers in 1927 (445 first class, 50 third class).]

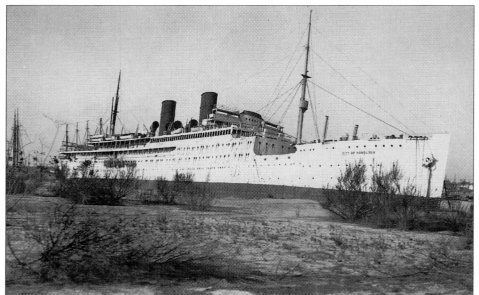

KROONLAND. The two sisterships *Kroonland* (**opposite, bottom**) and *Finland* were built at Philadelphia in 1902 for the Red Star Line. Under the U.S. flag they sailed the North Atlantic between New York and Antwerp. The *Kroonland* was transferred to the Belgian flag between 1908 and 1911. Both ships survived service in the First World War and then resumed sailing for Red Star. They were sold to the American Line in 1923 and then, within months, to the Panama Pacific Line for service between New York, Los Angeles, and San Francisco via the Panama Canal. The *Kroonland* finished her days at the hands of shipbreakers at Genoa, Italy, in 1927; the *Finland* was scrapped in Scotland a year later. [Built by William Cramp Shipbuilders, Philadelphia, Pennsylvania, 1902. 12,760 gross tons; 600 feet long; 60 feet wide. Steam triple-expansion engines, twin screw. Service speed 15 knots. 1,428 passengers by 1919 (242 first class, 310 second class, 876 third class).]

COLUMBIA. Another Red Star liner that eventually passed into American ownership was the three-funnel *Belgenland*. She was launched on December 31, 1914, after the First War had started, and then redesigned as a large cargo ship for the British government. She was completed in June 1917 as the *Belgic* for the British-flag White Star Line. A year later she was refitted as a troopship with 3,000 berths. In 1921–22 she was rebuilt as a passenger liner, entering service as the *Belgenland* in March 1923. Her around-the-world cruises were well known in the 1920s, running as long as 133 days and calling at sixty ports in fourteen countries. In 1933, during the Depression, she was laid up, then revived briefly, then laid up again. In early 1935 she was sold to American interests, the Atlantic Transport Company, renamed *Columbia*, and repainted with an all-white hull. She was used at first in the Panama Pacific Line's service between New York and California. But these sailings soon proved to be unprofitable, and she was sent off on mostly bargain-priced voyages to the Caribbean, Miami, and Bermuda. She also made sailings "to nowhere," short overnight excursions priced from $25. She was a familiar sight in New York Harbor (**above**). In 1935 she was laid up, "nested" alongside the far larger *Leviathan* at Pier 4 in Hoboken. In 1936, the *Columbia* set sail for Bo'ness in Scotland and the scrappers. [Built by Harland & Wolff Limited, Belfast, Northern Ireland, 1914–17. 24,578 gross tons; 697 feet long; 78 feet wide. Steam triple-expansion engines, triple screw. Service speed 17 knots. 2,600 passengers (500 first class, 600 second class, 1,500 third class).]

CHAPTER 3

Standard Classes

"These ships, especially the 535s and the 502s, were the lifeblood of the U.S. Merchant Marine and its revival after the First World War," declared Frank Braynard. "They were intended to be wartime troopers, but instead they saw commercial service from the start. They were remarkable examples of the tools of war becoming the tools of peace."

There were sixteen 535s and seven 502s, all named for their respective lengths. All were quite ordinary ships, built without frills on an accelerated wartime schedule. Although they lacked the finery and high style of the big luxury liners, they were solid and sturdy and became the mainstays of several American shipping lines. In operation they were a practical combination of limited accommodations for passengers and good-sized cargo holds. Best remembered are the *President Harding* and the *President Roosevelt,* both of which sailed on the North Atlantic for the prestigious United States Lines. Despite their large freight capacity, these ships were run more as passenger liners than freighters. Among other companies that made use of them were the Dollar Line (later American President Lines), the

American Mail Line, and the Munson Line. Most of these standard liners had long, productive lives. The last of the 535s, the *President Wilson,* finished sailng in 1958 as a Spanish vessel, *Cabo de Hornos.*

Some of the smaller ships were operated by companies such as the American Merchant Line, the Baltimore Mail Steamship Company, and the American Scantic Line. They carried passengers, too, usually in only one class, but often seemed more like freighters. When they docked next to the likes of the *Washington,* the *Paris,* or the *Rex,* they seemed by comparison to be like little toys. Whatever their size, they did yeoman service around the world. The *American Banker,* for instance, was built in 1919 to carry a standard dozen passengers. Sailing for the American Merchant Line, she was later modified to carry seventy-four. After World War II, renamed the *Arosa Kulm* by the Arosa Line, she had the capacity to carry well over 900 passengers. She was finally scrapped in 1959, one of the last of a line of war babies that had been put to good use by commercial operators in peacetime.

PRESIDENT ROOSEVELT (1922). The best-known and most-remembered of the so-called 535s were the sisters *President Roosevelt* and *President Harding*. They sailed on the North Atlantic between New York, Plymouth, Cherbourg, and Hamburg. While hardly luxurious superliners, they were typical combination passenger-cargo ships of the period. The *President Roosevelt* was launched in July 1922 as the *Peninsular State (above).* The following February she began her career on the Atlantic for the United States Lines, but was renamed *President Pierce* the following May and *President Roosevelt* a month later. She was enlisted in war service in 1940, first for the U.S. Army and then for the Navy as the USS *Joseph T. Dickman.* Withdrawn in early 1946, she was laid up with little chance of further service. In 1948 she was broken up at Oakland, California. The *President Harding* was completed as the *Lone Star State* in the spring of 1922, then renamed *President Taft* and *President Harding* the following summer. She was sold in 1940 to Belgian buyers and renamed *Ville de Bruges.* That career was cut short, however, when she was sunk on May 14, 1941, at the mouth of the River Schelde by Nazi bombers. [*President Roosevelt:* Built by New York Shipbuilding Corporation, Camden, New Jersey, 1922. 13,869 gross tons; 535 feet long; 65 feet wide. Steam turbines, twin screw. Service speed 17 knots. 437 passengers (201 cabin class, 236 third class).]

The public areas on many of the troopships converted to civilian use in the 1920s were decorated in the style of private clubs of the time. The Social Hall in cabin class on board the *President Roosevelt* **(left)** included a fireplace and grand piano.

PRESIDENT MADISON. Many of the 535s saw service in the Pacific. The *Bay State*, completed in late 1920, sailed between Seattle and Yokohama for the Admiral Oriental Line. In 1922 she was renamed *President Madison* and later assigned to the American Mail Line. She was nearly lost on March 24, 1933, when she heeled over at a Seattle shipyard berth *(above)*. She was righted three weeks later, but repairs took six months in all. She was sold to foreign buyers, the Manila-based Philippine Mail Line, in 1939 and renamed *President Quezon*. Her sailing days were cut short quite quickly, however, when she stranded on the Ryukyu Islands in January 1940—on her delivery voyage to the Philippines—and was wrecked. Afterward, the invading Japanese forces raised the wreckage and had it towed to Japan for demolition. [Built by the New York Shipbuilding Corporation, Camden, New Jersey, 1920. 14,187 gross tons; 535 feet long; 65 feet wide. Steam turbines, twin screw. Service speed 17 knots. 560 passengers (260 first class, 300 third class).]

AMERICAN LEGION. In this interesting aerial photograph *(opposite, top)*, dated November 29, 1939, three American standard-class passenger ships are seen moored together at the Todd Shipyard in Erie Basin, Brooklyn. At the top right the *President Roosevelt* is seen nested with another passenger ship of the United States Lines, the *American Trader*. An unidentified Belgian freighter and a Standard Oil tanker, the *J. A. Mowinckel*, are in the floating drydocks, while in the foreground the former Munson Line passenger ship *American Legion* is being readied for service as a military transport. The *American Legion*, which had been laid down in October 1919 as the troopship USS *Koda*, was completed in the summer of 1921 for Munson and used on their New York–South America service to Rio de Janeiro, Santos, Montevideo, and with a turnaround at Buenos Aires. She had three identical sisters on the same run, the *Southern Cross*, *Pan America*, and *Western World*. The Munson Line failed in July 1938, and their South American services were taken over by the newly formed American Republics Line, with their trio of large, luxurious ships, the *Argentina*, the *Brazil*, and the *Uruguay*. The four Munson passenger ships were taken over by the U.S. Maritime Commission and then went into government transport service. The *American Legion* survived the Second World War but was laid up at Astoria, Oregon, in April 1947. She was considered too old for further service and consequently was sold to scrappers at nearby Portland in May 1948. [Built by New York Shipbuilding Corporation, Camden, New Jersey, 1921. 13,737 gross tons; 535 feet long; 72 feet wide. Steam turbines, twin screw. Service speed 17 knots. 550 passengers (250 first class, 300 third class).]

ZEILIN. Shown *(opposite, bottom)* in her World War II garb as the Navy transport USS *Zeilin*, surrounded by small landing craft, this ship had been the *President Jackson* of the American Mail Line. She was used in transpacific passenger service, sailing from Seattle and Victoria, British Columbia, to Yokohama, Kobe, Shanghai, Hong Kong, and Manila. After 1937, however, American Mail discontinued its passenger operations and instead concentrated on freighters. The *Jackson* was laid up in July 1938 but resumed sailing in July 1940 as the *Zeilin* for the U.S. Navy. After being decommissioned in July 1946, she reverted to the name *President Jackson* and was sent to the "reserve fleet" in the James River, Virginia. She was soon released by the Government for disposal and was scrapped at Wilmington, Delaware, in May 1948. [Built by Newport News Shipbuilding & Drydock Company, Newport News, Virginia, 1921. 14,123 gross tons; 535 feet long; 65 feet wide. Steam turbines, twin screw. Service speed 17 knots. 560 passengers (260 first class, 300 third class).]

MARIGOLD. The USS *Marigold*, seen (*opposite, top*) during her service as a U.S. Navy hospital ship (1943–1946), was completed as the *Old North State* in late 1920. She was one of the smaller 502 class, a series of passenger-cargo ships that were 502 feet long between perpendiculars and 516 feet long overall. She was transferred to the United States Lines in 1921 and became the *President Van Buren*, then was sold to the San Francisco-based Dollar Line in 1924. Thereafter, she sailed in westward around-the-world service: 100-day voyages from New York to Havana, Cristóbal, Balboa, Los Angeles, San Francisco, Honolulu, Yokohama, Kobe, Shanghai, Hong Kong, Manila, Singapore, Penang, Colombo, Bombay, Suez, Port Said, Alexandria, Naples, Genoa, and Marseilles before returning to New York. In the late 1930s fares started at $815 for cabins without private bathroom facilities and from $900 for staterooms with toilet and shower. The *President Van Buren* often ran into problems, however. She went aground off Kobe in May 1925, was damaged by an engine room fire off Singapore in December 1929, and collided with the freighter *Oneida* off Boston in July 1932. When she was finally decommissioned from hospital ship service as the *Marigold* in 1946, she was laid up in the "reserve fleet" at Suisun Bay, California. She was broken up at nearby Oakland two years later. [Built by New York Shipbuilding Corporation, Camden, New Jersey, 1920. 10,533 gross tons; 516 feet long; 62 feet wide. Steam triple-expansion engines, twin screw. Service speed 14 knots. 78 all-first-class passengers.]

CABO DE HORNOS. The Spanish-flag *Cabo de Hornos* (*opposite, bottom*) was the last of the 535 and 502 classes by the time she was scrapped at Aviles, Spain, in 1959. She had been owned by the Ybarra Line and was used between Barcelona and ports along the east coast of South America. Originally, she had been completed as the *Empire State* in 1921, then was renamed *President Wilson* a year later by the Dollar Line. She was sold to the Spanish just after World War II started, in 1940, and was first named *Maria Pipa* and then *Cabo de Hornos*. A sistership, the *President Lincoln*, which had been launched as the *Hoosier State*, was also sold to the Spanish in 1940. She became the *Maria del Carmen*, a name soon changed to *Cabo de Buena Esperanza* by Ybarra & Company. She was scrapped in 1958, one year before her sistership. [Built by New York Shipbuilding Corporation, Camden, New Jersey, 1920. 14,127 gross tons; 535 feet long; 65 feet wide. Steam turbines, twin screw. Service speed 17 knots. 835 passengers in first and third class in 1953.]

AMERICAN FARMER. Among the smallest of North Atlantic passenger ships were the seven sisters of the *American Merchant* class. They ran service between New York and London, but had originally been freighters, built at Hog Island, Pennsylvania, and therefore known as "Hog Islanders." The *American Farmer* (*above*) had been named the *Ourcq* at launch in 1920, but was renamed in 1924, when she began London sailings for the American Merchant Line with newly fitted berths for twelve passengers. In 1926 this capacity was extended to seventy-four travelers, all in one-class quarters. She and her sisters were transferred to the United States Lines in 1931. She was sold in 1940 to an American-controlled, Belgian-flag company that bypassed the restrictions of the Neutrality Act. Renamed *Ville de Liege*, she was sunk by a German U-boat in April 1941. [Built by American Shipbuilding Corporation, Hog Island, Pennsylvania, 1920. 7,430 gross tons; 448 feet long; 58 feet wide. Steam turbines, single screw. Service speed 15 knots. 74 one-class passengers.]

CITY OF HAMBURG. The Baltimore Mail Steamship Company was created in 1930 to establish a passenger-cargo service between Baltimore and North European ports (via Norfolk to Le Havre, London, and Hamburg). Five World War I transports were purchased and given refits that included lengthening their hulls, installing new turbines, and adding berths for eighty passengers, all tourist class. The former transport *Eclipse*, for example, became the *City of Hamburg* and began Atlantic crossings in October 1931. The service lasted until 1938, when the five ships were transferred to the Panama Pacific Line for operation between New York, Los Angeles, and San Francisco via the Panama Canal. The *City of Hamburg* was renamed *City of San Francisco, (above).* She became the Navy transport USS *William P. Biddle* in 1940, was laid up in 1946, and finally went to the scrappers in 1957. [Built by Bethlehem Alameda Shipyard, Alameda, California, 1918. 8,424 gross tons; 506 feet long; 56 feet wide. Steam turbines, single screw. Service speed 16 knots. 80 all-tourist-class passengers.]

SCANYORK. In 1923 the American Scantic Lines, a division of the Moore-McCormack Lines, decided to expand their freighter service to Scandinavia and offer passenger berths. Four of the company's freighters, all "Hog Islanders," were refitted to carry seventy-four travelers on a route between New York and Gothenburg, Copenhagen, Gdynia, Stockholm, Helsinki, and occasionally Leningrad. Prices were moderate in the late 1930s. The two-week crossing to Copenhagen, for example, was priced from $100. As on most freighters, only one class of service was offered. One of the ships, the *Scanyork* (formerly the transport *Schenectady*), is shown *(below)* departing from Jersey City in June 1932 on her maiden voyage. In the fall of 1939, just after World War II began, she was sold to Lloyd Brasileiro, who renamed her *Maua*. Sailing primarily in the peaceful waters off South America, she survived the war but was wrecked along the Brazilian coast in 1952. [Built by American International Shipbuilding Corporation, Hog Island, Pennsylvania, 1919. 5,163 gross tons; 410 feet long; 54 feet wide. Steam turbines, single screw. Service speed 13 knots. 74 one-class passengers.]

CHAPTER 4

The Late Twenties: Big New Liners

Like many other businesses, shipping experienced a boom in the 1920s. As more Americans became interested in travel, and as import-export trade increased, the capacity of American shipping became strained. In response to increased demand, the U.S. shipping industry decided to increase capacity. By the late 1920s four of the largest liners ever built in North America had been launched. They were in a class with the 20,100-ton *Minnesota* and *Dakota*, built in 1905-1905, but set new standards of seagoing luxury and comfort.

The first of these big new ships to go into service was the *Malolo*, which offered all-first-class, Atlantic-liner-style accommodations for just under 700 passengers on the Matson Line's San Francisco-Honolulu run beginning in late 1927. "The *Malolo* was the last major ship to be built with private funds," said Frank Braynard. "She was also the first new passenger liner to be designed by William Francis Gibbs [the famed naval architect who went on to create the acclaimed *Santa Rosa* class, the *America*, and finally the *United States*]. Gibbs designed advanced safety and compartmentation systems for the *Malolo*. On her trials in the western Atlantic she had a collision with a freighter that had an impact equal to that which had sent the *Titanic* to the bottom fifteen years earlier. The *Malolo* survived and sailed into New York harbor flooded with over 5,000 tons of sea water."

The *Malolo* normally made the crossing from California to Hawaii in five days, and the passengers loved every minute of the voyage. The ship was responsible for the creation of a tradition, "Boat Day," when the tourists were welcomed to Honolulu harbor by an escort of outrigger canoes, then presented with bright flower leis, all accompanied by endless choruses of "Aloha Oe." Many travelers chose to cross on the *Malolo*, luxuriate on the islands, and return on a later sailing. Tourism boomed, and Matson capitalized on its investment by buying the storied Moana Hotel and building the 400-room Royal Hawaiian Hotel on the beach at Waikiki.

New York-headquartered Panama Pacific Line was responsible for building the other three big liners of the 1920s. The sisterships *California*, *Virginia*, and *Pennsylvania* were all 20,300 tons and were powered by the world's first turboelectric engines. Designed as single-stackers, they were restyled before completion with an added dummy funnel to make them seem more massive. Panama Pacific had resumed its service from New York to Los Angeles and San Francisco through the Panama Canal in 1923. At first they sailed veteran steamers such as the *Manchuria* and the *Mongolia*, built in 1903-1904. But it was soon apparent that the market was ready for more up-to-date ships. The three new sisters each carried some 750 passengers in two classes for the two-week voyage. They also took on a lot of cargo, including California fruit for the East Coast markets. Some tour operators offered the option of going one way by sea and one way by overland rail.

Unfortunately, the coast-to-coast service did not work out over the long term. The Great Depression of the 1930s cut into both passenger and freight revenues, and operating expenses were increased by rising Panama Canal tolls and by strikes that led to wage increases. The service struggled through until the spring of 1938, when federal operating subsidies ended. The three big ships were then laid up and transferred to the U.S. Maritime Commision. Refitted with wide single stacks, they were assigned to the American Republics Line, but under the direct management of the Moore-McCormack Line. They were placed on the service from New York to the east coast of South America and, in line with President Franklin D. Roosevelt's Good Neighbor Policy, renamed *Uruguay* (ex-*California*), *Brazil* (ex-*Virginia*), and *Argentina* (ex-*Pennsylvania*). Their thirty-eight-day round trips took them as far south as Buenos Aires. According to Jack Weatherford, "Ships such as these strengthened U.S. relations with Latin America, especially Brazil and Argentina. The regular appearances of these ships created an American presence there."

MALOLO. The 17,232-ton *Malolo* was by far the largest and most luxurious passenger liner yet built for the California–Hawaii trade. She had splendid all-first-class accommodations with fine public spaces, and her success encouraged the San Francisco-based Matson Navigation Company to build no less than a trio of larger liners for Pacific service. Following her news-making collision, May 25, 1927, and near-sinking during trials in the western Atlantic, the *Malolo* was repaired and then sailed to the West Coast via Panama to take up her duties on the five-day run to Honolulu. She is seen (*above*) departing from New York on her delivery voyage to San Francisco on October 27, 1927. [Built by William Cramp Shipbuilders, Philadelphia, Pennsylvania, 1927. 17,232 gross tons; 582 feet long; 82 feet wide. Steam turbines, twin screw. Service speed 21 knots. 693 all-first-class passengers.]

The *Malolo's* main lounge (**below**) was a grand space, with a very spacious, comfortable look.

Late in 1937 the *Malolo* was extensively rebuilt so as to make her more compatible with the larger *Lurline* and her sisters, the *Mariposa* and *Monterey*, all of which were added by Matson in 1931–32. The *Malolo* had her lifeboats raised two decks and placed in up-to-date gravity davits, making room for a series of lanai suites. For her return to service in January 1938 Matson even gave her a new name: *Matsonia*

(**above**). With the beginning of the Second World War, she was pressed into service as a troopship. She briefly resumed Hawaiian service in 1946, then was sold two years later to the Panamanian-registered Home Lines, among the first of large American liners to go to foreign owners. Renamed *Atlantic*, she sailed between the Mediterranean and New York and later, out of northern European ports, to New York and eastern Canada. In late 1954 she raised the Greek colors when she joined a Home Lines subsidiary, the National Hellenic American Line, and became their *Queen Frederica*. Again, she was on the Mediterranean–New York route. Another Greek company, the Chandris Lines, bought her in 1965 for use on ocean crossings, cruises, and three-month tourist and immigrant voyages around the world. She was retired in 1973 and laid up in Greece. There were rumors of some further service, perhaps as a floating hotel along the Suez Canal, but nothing came to pass. In 1977 a film company wanted to use her as a "floating prop" in the film *Raise the Titanic*. She would have portrayed that tragic liner, but gradual demolition of her outer decks had already begun, and the production team chose another laid-up Greek passenger ship instead, the *Athinai*, the former *Santa Paula* (see Chapter 6). The former *Malolo* was deliberately set afire during her demolition so as to burn away the teak on her outer decks. Her last pieces were cut up during 1978, fifty-one years after her maiden voyage.

SANTA MARIA. The New York–headquartered Grace Line had strong interests in the Caribbean and west coast of South America trades. To strengthen their services from New York to Valparaiso via Kingston; Cristóbal, Balboa (Panama); Buenaventura, Guayaquil (Ecuador); Talaba, Salaverry, Callao, Mollendo (Peru); Arica, Iquique, Antofagasta, Chañaral, Coquimbo, San Antonio, and Talcahuano (Chile)—they added distinctive tonnage in the late 1920s. Two passenger-cargo liners, notable in being American-flag ships built in England, were also the first large U.S. passenger ships to be diesel-driven. The *Santa Maria* (*above*) was completed in the spring of 1928, while a twin sister, the *Santa Barbara*, followed that September. A near-sister named *Santa Clara*, added in April 1930, was built at the New York Shipbuilding Corporation, Camden, New Jersey. The *Santa Maria* carried 157 all-first-class passengers, and every cabin had private bathroom facilities. Fares in 1935 for the three-week voyage from New York to Valparaiso were $364 in a minimum stateroom to $1,390 in a suite (bedroom, living room, full bath). During the war the *Santa Maria* became the Navy troopship USS *Barnett*, and afterward, in 1948, she was sold to become the Italian immigrant ship *Surriento*. She was scrapped in 1965. [*Santa Maria*: built by Furness Shipbuilding Company, Haverton-on-Tees, England, 1928. 8,060 gross tons; 486 feet long; 64 feet wide. Diesels, twin screw. Service speed 16.5 knots. 157 all-first-class passengers.]

PENNSYLVANIA. In 1928 the Panama Pacific Line ordered three new liners, the largest yet for intercoastal service between New York, Los Angeles, and San Francisco via Panama. They were the world's first turboelectric liners. Initially designed with one funnel, they were built with two, the second being a "dummy" added for effect. The *California* was the first of this threesome to appear, in January 1928. The *Virginia* came in December 1928, the *Pennsylvania* in October 1929. Two of the ships are seen (*opposite*) with four other American passenger ships along New York City's Chelsea Piers in 1935. From top to bottom are the *American Shipper*, *President Roosevelt*, *Washington*, and *American Importer*, all of the United States Lines, and the *Pennsylvania* and *Virginia*. The Depression cut deeply into the success of these Panama Pacific liners, which were found to be too large for the intercoastal trade. When their federal operating subsidies ended, Panama Pacific managers decided to lay up the three ships at New York in March and April, 1938. Soon, however, they were handed over to the U.S. Maritime Commission and sent to Newport News for refitting. They were then reassigned to the newly formed American Republics Line for South American service. [Built by Newport News Shipbuilding & Drydock Company, Newport News, Virginia, 1929. 20,526 gross tons; 613 feet long; 80 feet wide. Steam turboelectric engines, twin screw. Service speed 17 knots. 750 passengers (385 first class, 365 tourist class).]

CALIFORNIA. American Republics, a division of Moore-McCormack Lines, decided to have the three Panama Pacific ships redesigned with a single, wide funnel. The *California* is seen (***right***) under reconstruction at Newport News. In preparation for their new service to the Southern Hemisphere, the liners were renamed: the *California* became the *Uruguay*; the *Virginia*, the *Brazil*; and the *Pennsylvania*, the *Argentina*. [Built by Newport News Shipbuilding Drydock Company, Newport News, Virginia, 1928. 20,325 gross tons; 601 feet long; 80 feet wide. Steam turboelectric engines, twinscrew. Service speed 17 knots. 747 passengers (384 first class, 363 tourist class).]

URUGUAY. The American Republics Line ran thirty-eight-day round-trip voyages out of New York to the east coast of South America, calling at Trinidad, Rio de Janeiro (where the *Uruguay* is shown in this 1938 view, *opposite, bottom*), Santos, Montevideo, and then turnaround at Buenos Aires. After duties as troopships in the Second World War, the *Uruguay* and her sisters were restored for further service to Latin America. The postwar refit for the *Uruguay* took longer than expected, however. Initially, the task was assigned to the Todd Shipyards in Brooklyn in November 1947. But that facility was soon paralyzed by a strike, and the 601-foot-long ship had to be shifted within the confines of New York Bay to the Federal Shipyards at Kearny, New Jersey. She returned to the South American run in February 1948.

Until 1954, when the *Uruguay* was withdrawn and laid up in the James River "reserve fleet" in Virginia, there was a South America-bound passenger ship sailing from New York every two weeks, usually at midday on Friday. After the war the American Republics coloring was discarded in favor of Moore-McCormack's own colors, which featured a large red "M" as a centerpiece. The ships used a Lower Manhattan berth, Pier 32, at the foot of Canal Street. In this aerial view *(above)* the *Argentina* is on the left, the *Brazil* (which is having a crew lifeboat drill) is to the right. A Ward Line freighter, the *Siboney*, is just across the slip, at Pier 34, from the *Argentina*. Ward did not resume passenger ship services after the Second World War. Long vacated by the likes of Moore-McCormack, Pier 32 was demolished in 1982.

The accommodations on board these Moore-McCormack liners were divided into two classes: On the *Brazil*, it was 234 in first class and 185 in cabin class. That ship's first-class main lounge is shown in this 1948 view (**right**).

The large first-class dining room (**right**) had an open well area in the center section and was air conditioned. The cabin-class restaurant was similarly cooled, but all other areas on board used forced-air ventilation. The *Uruguay* was laid up in 1954, and the *Argentina* and the *Brazil* joined her in the James River "mothball fleet" by the end of 1958. The *Brazil* and the *Argentina* were scrapped by the former Federal Shipyards at Kearny in 1964; the *Uruguay* at a small plant at Bordentown, New Jersey, that same year.

CHAPTER 5

Small Ships of the Prewar Era

An often-forgotten part of U.S. maritime history is the story of the "little liners," which had their heyday in the 1920s and '30s. Many of them had style, accommodations, and service that were equal to the amenities provided by the famous transatlantic liners. The *Iroquois* and *Shawnee*, for example, even had two stacks, which gave them a "big ship" appearance.

"They were important ships, a wonderful fleet in themselves," remembered Frank Braynard. "And they were especially valuable during the Second World War. They were tiny liners in every way, but they were elegant and comfortable, offering pleasant voyages. During the Depression, in particular, their short, often inexpensive sailings were the ideal 'getaways,' escapes from the worrisome times at home. But few of them returned to service after the war. Among other problems, these ships were undervalued. By 1946-47 they were worth much less than in 1939. Happily, however, some saw further service for foreign-flag lines—such as the *Iroquois*, which became the Turkish *Ankara* in 1948."

Before the war these ships had provided service on a variety of lines—New York to Portland (Maine), to Norfolk, to Miami, to San Juan, and to New Orleans. A major owner of little liners on the East Coast during the 1920s and '30s was the AGWI Lines (Atlantic & Gulf & West Indies Steamship Company), which eventually included the Ward, Porto Rico, Clyde Mallory, and other lines. Clyde Mallory was itself the result of a merger in 1928 of the Clyde Line, founded in 1886, and the Mallory Steamship Company, dating from 1876. Among their major ships were the *Iroquois* and the *Algonquin*. AGWI resumed sailing after World War II but was unable to weather the changing economics of the U.S. shipping industry, and went into bankruptcy in July 1953. A similar fate overtook another company in the East Coast trade, Merchants & Miners Transportation Company. They had begun operations way back in 1852 with service between Baltimore and Boston (at that time the second and third largest cities, respectively, in the U.S.). Another important East Coast company was the Eastern Steamship Lines, described more fully on page 32 with one of their flagships, the *Acadia*. They effectively ceased operations in New England just a few years after the end of World War II.

The Pacific coastal trades were never as large or diverse as those along the East Coast. Nevertheless, many steamers ran between such ports as Los Angeles, San Francisco, Seattle, and north to Alaska (see page 40 for coverage of the Alaskan Steamship Company). A well-known firm in the West was the Admiral Line, which was founded in 1916. Like many others, they ran into financial problems after the 1929 Crash and in 1933 were merged into the Dollar Line. Unfortunately, Dollar soon faced its own financial problems and had to be reorganized as the American President Lines in 1938.

Many small ships served the nation well during World War II. But after the war, with the boom in construction of superhighways for trucks as well as autos, along with the rise in competition from foreign-flag carriers as well as rapidly growing airlines, soon overwhelmed these ships and their services. When the aforementioned *Ankara* was demolished on the beaches of Aliaga, Turkey, she had been just about the last survivor of these small American gems of the ocean.

Decommissioned in 1946, she was sold to the Turkish Maritime Lines and renamed *Ankara*. Used as a full-time cruiseship in later years, she was laid up in 1977 and then broken up at Aliaga in November 1981. The *Shawnee*, used as a trooper in the war, was sold in 1946 to become the Panama-flag *City of Lisbon* and, in 1947, the Yugoslavian *Partizanka*. She was destroyed by fire at Split on the Adriatic Sea, September 13, 1949. [*Iroquois*: Built by Newport News Shipbuilding & Drydock Company, Newport News, Virginia, 1927. 6,209 gross tons; 409 feet long; 62 feet wide. Steam turbines, twin screw. Service speed 17 knots. 754 passengers (640 first class, 114 steerage).]

ALGONQUIN. The Clyde Line built four new sisterships just before the larger *Iroquois* and *Shawnee*. Their names were *Cherokee*, *Seminole*, *Mohawk*, and *Algonquin*, and they were used on the services from New York to Charleston, Jacksonville, and Miami. The *Algonquin* made news when she rammed and sank the Furness-Bermuda Line passenger ship *Fort Victoria* off New York's Ambrose Light on December 18, 1929. Then on July 3, 1940, she caught fire and partially sank at Clyde Mallory's New York Pier 34 (**opposite, top**). Later repaired, she was used as a hospital ship during the war and then decommissioned in 1946. Like almost all other coastal passenger ships, she was not restored for commercial service but sat out the next decade in the James River. She was broken up at Baltimore in 1957. [Built by Newport News Shipbuilding & Drydock Company, Newport News, Virginia, 1926. 5,945 gross tons; 402 feet long; 55 feet wide. Steam turbines, single screw. Service speed 16 knots. 446 passengers (421 first class, 25 steerage).]

ACADIA. The Boston-based Eastern Steamship Lines was formed in 1905 for passenger services in New England and the Canadian Maritime Provinces. Among their subsidiaries were some of the area's oldest shipowners. The Boston & Bangor Steamship Company, for example, was formed in 1834, the Portland Steam Packet Company in 1843, and the International Steamship Company in 1859. The Eastern combine later included the likes of the Metropolitan Steamship Company and, in 1923, the Old Dominion Line, as its passenger services included New York and extended the entire length of the East Coast. They built new ships for summer services to Canada and then Caribbean charters in winter. With all the grace of miniature ocean liners, the first of these, the *Yarmouth* and the *Evangeline*, were added in 1927. Highly successful at the start, they were followed by two larger, improved near-sisters, the *Saint John* and the *Acadia*. But the Depression adversely affected all coastal passenger ship operators, and the *Acadia* was the last coastwise liner built in the United States. She is seen (**opposite, bottom**) in May 1937, undergoing her annual refit in Bethlehem Steel's Simpson Works, East Boston.

On her summertime sailings the *Acadia* would depart from New York's Pier 18 at ten o'clock on Monday mornings and reach Yarmouth, Nova Scotia, at eight-thirty the following morning. She would then sail again from New York on Thursdays. A minimum inside two-berth room was priced at $2.50 ($1 for the upper berth, $1.50 for the lower bunk); $13.50 per person bought the finest cabin on board. [Built by Newport News Shipbuilding & Drydock Company, Newport News, Virginia, 1932. 6,185 gross tons; 403 feet long; 51 feet wide. Steam turbines, twin screw. Service speed 20 knots. 750 passengers in first and second class.]

IROQUOIS. Two of the largest and perhaps grandest of the American intercoastal liners were the sisters *Iroquois* and *Shawnee*, which were completed just weeks apart in the summer of 1927. Their graceful appearances were capped by twin funnels, which gave them something of the style of an Atlantic luxury liner in miniature. The ships were barely over 6,200 tons in size and little more than 400 feet in length. They were owned by the New York-based Clyde Mallory Lines. The maiden voyage for the *Iroquois* was from New York to Boston, Halifax, and Quebec City, but she was normally intended to sail to Florida ports, namely Jacksonville and Miami, and on occasional tropic cruises. In 1935 the two-night voyage from New York to Miami was priced from $45 one way or from $65 for a round trip. In the winter of 1935–36 the *Iroquois* made six thirteen-day cruises from New York to Miami, Port-au-Prince, Kingston, Havana, Miami, and then return to New York. Fares started at $115. A six-day New York–Miami cruise was available at a cost of $65.

In the fall of 1939 the *Iroquois* joined several coastal liners (including the *Orizaba*, the *Shawnee*, the *St. John*, and the *Acadia*) for evacuation voyages out of Europe. This photo (**above**) shows the ship some 150 miles west of American shores, on October 11, 1939, carrying 776 passengers and crew bound for New York. She was given a U.S. Navy escort after word was received that Nazi U-boats planned to sink her. Note the American flags painted on the canopy over the bridge.

The *Iroquois* was bought by the U.S. Navy in July 1940 and converted (with her second funnel removed) to the hospital ship *Solace*. She was at Pearl Harbor on December 7, 1941, but survived intact.

The *Acadia* was taken over by the U.S. Army in December 1941 for use as a troopship, then was refitted as a hospital ship nine months later. She is seen in hospital white (*opposite, top*) steaming into harbor. After the war she was laid up, but even if Eastern Steamship Lines had been interested in restoring her for commercial sailings, shipyard refit costs had skyrocketed by the late 1940s. Foreign interests had a look at the ship, but she remained in the James River fleet until sold to scrappers in Belgium in 1955. She was towed across the Atlantic to Bruges and broken up.

EVANGELINE. Only two of Eastern's prewar passenger ships, the sisters *Yarmouth* and *Evangeline*, resumed service in 1947, sailing on the old service up to Nova Scotia. But increasing operational costs combined with a loss in summertime trade made the ships unprofitable, at least under the U.S. flag. After long layups they were sold to the Eastern Steamship Company of Miami and changed to flags of convenience—the *Yarmouth* hoisting the Panamanian flag, the *Evangeline*, Liberian colors. Running two-to-fourteen-day cruises out of Miami to the Bahamas and the Caribbean, they were forerunners of the huge Florida cruise trade. Today Miami is the world's busiest cruise port.

The *Yarmouth* went on to become the *Yarmouth Castle, Queen of Nassau, Yarmouth Castle, Yarmouth, San Andres,* and in her final days *Elizabeth A.* Laid up in Greece in 1967, she was scrapped there in 1979. The *Evangeline* retained her original name almost to the very end. She is seen (*opposite, bottom*) in a view dated October 21, 1961. She was renamed *Yarmouth Castle* in 1964, then burned and sank on November 13, 1965, while on a short cruise from Miami to Nassau. Eighty-nine perished in the highly publicized tragedy, which brought about far more stringent safety standards for all passenger ship operators using U.S. ports and carrying American passengers. [Built by William Cramp Shipbuilders, Philadelphia, Pennsylvania, 1927. 5,043 gross tons; 378 feet long; 65 feet wide. Steam turbines, twin screw. Service speed 18 knots. 751 passengers as built (589 first class, 162 second class).]

COLOMBIA. The Colombian Steamship Company was formed in 1923 to take over the Clyde Line's services to the West Indies and South America. The fleet was composed of eight freighters. But by 1932 it had been reorganized as the Colombian Mail Steamship Corporation, generally called the Colombian Line, and added two passenger ships, the 5,200-ton sisters *Colombia* (shown [*above*] at New York on her maiden sailing, November 21, 1932) and the *Haiti.* Costing some $5 million each, they were handsome little passenger-cargo ships that offered eighteen-day round-trip voyages to Port-au-Prince, Kingston, Puerto Colombia, Cartagena, Cristóbal, and then homeward via Kingston, Port-au-Prince, and Cap Haitien. The round trip was priced at $210 per person by 1937 and at $500 per person in the ships' deluxe suites (bedroom, private verandah and full bath). Together with the chartered *Pastores* of United Fruit, one ship sailed every Thursday at twelve noon from Pier 8 in Brooklyn Heights. When the ships returned to New York, they arrived at Pier 20 in Manhattan, on the East River.

By 1937 the Colombian Line closed down, defeated by competition from the larger Grace and Ward lines as well as the Dutch-flag Royal Netherlands Steamship Company. The two ships were transferred to the AGWI Lines, which shifted them to subsidiaries: the *Colombia* went to the Ward Line and became the *Mexico,* while the *Haiti* was renamed *Puerto Rico.* Both ships survived World War II, then were sold to the Turkish Maritime Lines, joining the former *Iroquois* as well as American Export's one-time *Exochorda.* The *Mexico* sailed in the Mediterranean as the *Istanbul* until broken up in 1966; the *Puerto Rico* was transferred to the Ward Line in 1939 and became the *Monterey* (with the Matson Line's *Monterey* of 1932, there were now two passenger ships of the same name under the U.S. flag). The old *Monterey* was sold to the Turks in 1946 and was called *Adana* until scrapped in 1967. [Built by Newport News Shipbuilding & Drydock Company, Newport News, Virginia, 1932. 5,236 gross tons; 404 feet long; 58 feet wide. Steam turbines, single screw. Service speed 17 knots. 125 passengers as built (101 first class, 24 tourist class).]

AROSA STAR. Another of the long-lasting vessels among the smaller American passenger ships was the former *Borinquen*. She was built and operated by the Porto Rico Line, and traded between New York and the eastern Caribbean. Used as a trooper in the war, she was one of the few that resumed sailing in the late 1940s, first for the AGWI Lines and then, after being sold to the Bull Line in 1949, as the *Puerto Rico*. She was laid up in 1953, then sold to the Swiss-owned Arosa Line a year later and renamed *Arosa Star* *(above)*. Fully refitted, the 200 all-first-class berths of her Bull Line days were changed to thirty-eight in first class and 768 in a crowded tourist class. She was fitted with a new raked bow and lengthened by as much as 38 feet. After the refit, which cost $1 million, in May 1954 she began sailing from Bremerhaven, Le Havre, and Southampton to Quebec City and Montreal, with occasional sailings to Halifax and New York as well as periodic cruises. Arosa went bankrupt in 1958, and the *Arosa Star* was "arrested" at Bermuda for debts. She was auctioned off for $510,000 to Eastern Steamship Lines. Renamed *Bahama Star*, she began three- and four-day cruises between Miami and Nassau, with fares starting at $59. This run paved the way for today's highly successful service, when cruise ships of over 70,000 tons carry as many as 2,600 passengers each.

When the *Bahama Star* could no longer pass U.S. Coast Guard safety inspections, she was laid up in November 1968. She was then renamed *La Janelle* and brought out to California for conversion to a floating hotel. But on April 13, 1970, she capsized in a hurricane at Port Hueneme, and had to be scrapped. [Built by Bethlehem Steel Company, Quincy, Massachusetts, 1931. 9,070 gross tons; 466 feet long; 60 feet wide. Steam turbines, single screw. Service speed 15 knots. 806 passengers (38 first class, 768 tourist class).]

DIXIE. The largest, finest, and in fact the last passenger ship for the Morgan Line, an arm of the Southern Pacific Railroad, was the *Dixie*. On round-trip voyages between New York and New Orleans, she would sail from Manhattan's Pier 49 on Wednesday afternoon, reach New Orleans six days later, and spend four days there before returning to New York for a Thursday morning arrival. A brochure in the mid-1930s advertised that the *Dixie* "offers deluxe passenger service to New Orleans and connecting there with the Sunset Limited, the Argonaut, and other air-conditioned trains for the southwest, Mexico, and the Pacific Coast." One-way fares began at $75. The *Dixie* was nearly lost during a hurricane, when she went aground on French Reef in the Florida Keys, September 2, 1935 *(opposite, top)*. She was refloated seventeen days later and towed to the Todd Shipyard in Brooklyn for extensive repairs. The Morgan Line service ended when the *Dixie* was sold to the U.S. Navy in 1941. Renamed USS *Alcor*, she was later converted to a repair ship and then to a destroyer tender. Decommissioned by 1946, she was scrapped at Baltimore in 1950. [Built by Federal Shipbuilding & Drydock Company, Kearny, New Jersey, 1927. 8,188 gross tons; 445 feet long; 60 feet wide. Steam turbines, single screw. Service speed 16 knots. 379 passengers (279 first class, 100 third class).]

BERKSHIRE. Merchants & Miners Transportation Company dated from 1852, when they established a service between Baltimore and Boston. Over the years they became a major factor in the coastal passenger ship trade. As part of their rebuilding program after the First World War, they ordered five sisterships. The *Allegheny* and the *Berkshire* came from the Federal Shipyards in New Jersey in 1923; the *Chatham*, the *Dorchester*, and the *Fairfax* were built at Newport News and commissioned in 1926. They ran from Boston, Baltimore, and Philadelphia to Savannah, Jacksonville, and Miami. Fares from Boston to Miami were $49 in first class and $31 in tourist. With the great changes in the coastal trade after the Second World War, Merchants & Miners was liquidated in 1948. The *Berkshire*, shown *(opposite, bottom)* during a cruise to Nassau in 1941, was soon converted to a government-owned training ship, the *American Engineer*. She was scrapped at San Francisco in 1948. [Built by Federal Shipbuilding & Drydock Company, Kearny, New Jersey, 1923. 5,486 gross tons; 368 feet long; 52 feet wide. Steam turbines, single screw. Service speed 12 knots. 302 passengers (275 first class, 27 steerage).]

FLORIDA. Florida's Peninsular & Occidental Steamship Company (P&O), dating from 1900 and originally formed by the Florida East Coast Railroad and the Atlantic Coast Line Railroad for services from Miami to Nassau and Havana via Key West, is probably best remembered for their *Florida (opposite)*, a ship that sailed from 1931 until 1966. She was also a pioneer of today's multibillion-dollar Florida cruise business. The old *Florida* offered some of the first continuous cruises from the port of Miami. Initially, however, she was built for the Key West–Havana service. But in 1934 a hurricane destroyed the terminal at Key West, and the sailings of the *Florida* were moved to Miami. A cruise service to Nassau was attempted in 1954, but the ship soon returned to the Havana run, only to return to Bahamas service after the Castro regime closed Cuba to cruise ships by 1960. The *Florida* was replaced in November 1966 by the chartered Israeli passenger ship *Jerusalem* (renamed *Miami*), then she was sold to become the *New Bahama Star* for the rival Eastern Steamship Lines. P&O then ceased operations. Shown while boarding a pilot off Hog Island in the Bahamas in the mid-1950s (with her homeport, quite uniquely, shown as New Haven, Connecticut), the *Florida* herself was used as a floating hotel at Expo 67 at Montreal and then offered for sale. But only scrap merchants were interested, and so the thirty-seven-year-old was towed across the Atlantic to Santander, Spain, for demolition. [Built by Newport News Shipbuilding & Drydock Company, Newport News, Virginia, 1931. 4,923 gross tons; 387 feet long; 57 feet wide. Steam turbines, twin screw. Service speed 19 knots. 742 passengers (612 first class, 130 second class).]

H. F. ALEXANDER. The Pacific coastal trades were never as large or as diverse as those along the East Coast. A well-known firm in the West was the Admiral Line, which traded from 1916 until 1936. Their greatest ship was the *H. F. Alexander*, shown *(above)* at the Bethlehem Steel shipyard at San Francisco in the 1930s. The ship had been the *Great Northern*, owned by the Great Northern Pacific Steamship Company and used on the run between San Francisco, Astoria, and Portland. In winter she sailed to Hawaii. Used as a troopship in the First World War, she was retained by the U.S. Navy and recommissioned in 1921 as the USS *Columbia*. Admiral Line bought her a year later and refitted her as the *H. F. Alexander* for San Francisco–Seattle service. Her powerful engines earned her the nickname "the Galloping Ghost of the Pacific Ocean." She made the 807-mile run to Seattle in thirty-nine hours, three hours less than the railroads. In March 1924 she established her best record: thirty-seven hours, thirteen minutes.

The *Alexander's* original sistership, the *Northern Pacific*, remained a Navy transport after the First World War, and subsequently burned and sank off Cape May, New Jersey, in February 1922. The *H. F. Alexander* herself was laid up at San Francisco in September 1936, then was reactivated for use as a floating hotel for the Golden Gate World Exposition in San Francisco, in 1939. She was restored for service by the Army in 1942 and became the troopship USS *George S. Simonds*. Laid up afterward, she was soon declared surplus and was broken up at Philadelphia in 1948. [Built by William Cramp Shipbuilders, Philadelphia, Pennsylvania, 1915. 8,255 gross tons; 525 feet long; 63 feet wide. Steam turbines, triple screw. Service speed 23 knots. 850 passengers as built.]

ALEUTIAN. The Alaskan Steamship Company ran passenger and freighter services out of Seattle and other Pacific Northwest ports up to Alaska on what was known as one of the most hazardous ocean routes of all. The *Aleutian* (*above*) had been built in 1906 as the *Mexico* for the New York-based Ward Line. She was bought by ASC in 1929 and moved out to the Pacific. They kept her sailing until 1953. She was then chartered to the short-lived Hawaiian-Pacific Line, who hoped to compete with the well-established Matson Line for the California-Hawaii trade. Various problems intervened, however, and her maiden sailing never came about. Sixteen months later, in November 1954, she was sold to the Caribbean-Atlantic Line. They renamed her *Tradewind* and placed her under the Liberian flag. She ran cruises from Miami, Washington, D.C., and even from Richmond, Virginia, but with little financial success. She was finally "arrested" for debts totaling $550,000 and then auctioned off to Baltimore scrappers, who in turn resold her to Belgian shipbreakers. She was demolished at Ghent in 1956. [Built by William Cramp Shipbuilders, Philadelphia, Pennsylvania, 1906. 6,207 gross tons; 416 feet long; 50 feet wide. Steam turbines, twin screw. Service speed 17 knots. Approximately 250 passengers.]

MAZATLÁN. Another of Alaska Steamship's elderly passenger ships that attempted to find further life after sailing the Inside Passage for decades was the 1923-built *Alaska*. She was sold in 1955 to the newly created Margo-Pacific Lines, who renamed her *Mazatlán* (*below*). With barely a refit and no improvement or modification for tropical service, she was sent on twelve-day inexpensive "tourist cruises" from San Diego to Mazatlán and Acapulco. The ship developed seemingly endless problems: mechanical breakdowns, crew difficulties, and sweltering conditions on board. She even broke down on her inaugural cruise and had to be towed back to San Diego. In the end her owners went bankrupt, and the ship was auctioned off in January 1956 to Japanese scrap merchants for just over $171,000. [Built by Todd Shipyards, Seattle, Washington, 1923. 4,515 gross tons; 366 feet long; 50 feet wide. Steam turbines, twin screw. Service speed 16 knots. Approximately 220 passengers.]

CHAPTER 6

Expansion: Building Up the Fleet

Passenger ship travel began to decline after the Crash of 1929. Shipowners, desperate for any source of revenue, often sent their vessels off on inexpensive short cruises. A long weekend from New York to Halifax and back on the United States Lines' new *Manhattan*, for instance, was priced at $49 in the mid-1930s. "It was mostly schoolteachers and office workers who sailed in those days," recalled New York ocean liner observer John Gillespie. "They at least had the steady salaries that allowed for a vacation, even a short one. A quick cruise up to Nova Scotia or down to Bermuda was ideal. And it all introduced passenger ship travel, in fact, cruising, to people who never would have sailed otherwise. It was the 1930s that brought cruising to the general public, to the middle class."

A good many luxury liners that had been designed and ordered in the booming twenties were delivered to their nervous new owners in the fizzling thirties. Among their number were the *Empress of Britain* for Canadian Pacific (1931), the *Rex* and the *Conte de Savoia* for the Italian Line (1932), the *Normandie* for the French Line (1935), and the *Queen Mary* for the Cunard Line (1936). Many of these ships had been built with government money and in anticipation of operating subsidies. U.S. maritime powers were more conservative in their approach. They still remembered that the *Leviathan* had been extraordinarily unsuccessful, so there seemed to be no reason to replace her with another white elephant. Instead, the Americans opted for a pair of 24,300-tonners, the *Manhattan* and the *Washington* of 1932-1933.

"The *Manhattan* and the *Washington*, two fine ships in their own right, actually revolutionized transatlantic travel in the 1930s," commented Frank Braynard. "They introduced cabin class [also called second class on some ships] and made it virtually equal to first class. It became very popular. Cabin-class rates on first-class ships! It was all part of an effort to recruit more passengers during the Depression. First-class fares seemed too high, while cabin-class rates seemed affordable. It was quite a shocker at first for the United States Lines to do this, but soon other companies like the French Line followed. They introduced their 'cabin liners,' the *Lafayette* and the *Champlain*. It was all the brilliant idea of P. V. G. Mitchell, the vice president of passenger traffic for the United States Lines. The *Manhattan* and the *Washington* were superb in every way and outclassed all other American ships yet built."

American Export Lines, with headquarters in New York, made a bold move in 1931 by beginning transatlantic passenger service to ports in the Mediterranean. They built a quartet of handsome combination ships, *Excalibur*, *Excambion*, *Exeter*, and *Exochorda*, which became known as "the Four Aces." They each carried 125 guests in cabins outfitted with private baths and other amenities.

Another New York shipowner, the Grace Line, also added a foursome to their fleet in 1932—the *Santa Rosa* and her three sisters, the *Santa Paula*, the *Santa Lucia*, and the *Santa Elena*. These ships sailed from the East Coast to the West Coast, but with emphasis on the Caribbean and Panama Canal transit. They had superior accommodations, highlighted by an outdoor swimming pool and lido area. They also introduced a great novelty—a roll-back roof for the main reestaurant on the upper deck. Once in warm waters, passengers could dine under the tropic stars.

The United Fruit Company also took advantage of federal funds and built their finest passenger-cargo ships ever, the six sisters of the *Talamanca* class. Bearing a strong resemblance to large, gleaming-white yachts, they catered to no more than 100 all-first-class passengers. Another company with an interest in sailings to the tropics was the Ward Line, which took delivery on their finest liners, the 11,500-ton *Morro Castle* and *Oriente*, in 1930. Ward ran a popular weekly service between New York and Havana, Cuba. Unfortunately, the *Morro Castle*, considered to be the last word in American ship construction and with the highest advances in marine safety, was involved in a highly publicized tragedy: 123 people died when a fire burned out of control and virtually destroyed the great ship as it sailed along the New Jersey coast.

Competition was another reason for building new liners. In the Pacific Japan's NYK (Nippon Yusen Kaisha) Line in 1929-1930 added to its fleet three of its finest liners—the *Asama Maru*, the *Tatsuta Maru*, and the *Chichibu Maru*. To meet this challenge San Francisco's Dollar Line ordered the largest and most impressive liners America could provide. These were the first ships to be designed and built to Dollar's specifications. Previously, the line had either bought second-hand vessels or accepted new ships that had been designed as government transports. The luxurious new liners, the *President Hoover* and the *President Coolidge*, were put into service in August and November, respectively, of 1931.

Another San Francisco firm, Matson, also jumped on the expansion express. Savoring the success of their *Malolo*, they used federal construction subsidies to build three liners that were even larger than their flagship. The first two, the *Mariposa* and the *Monterey*, were ordered for Matson's South Pacific runs from California to Australia. The third ship, named *Lurline*, joined the *Malolo* on the increasingly popular cruises to Hawaii. These were exceptional ships, said to be among the most splendid of American liners. They proved to be enduring as well. The *Monterey* was still afloat in 1999, sixty-seven years after its launching in 1932. Like the *Monterey*, the Grace Line's *Santa Rosa* (1932) also had a long life, not being consigned to the scrap heap until 1989. Many others, however, either did not survive World War II or were scrapped as passenger traffic declined in the postwar era.

MANHATTAN. Down the ways at Camden! The *Manhattan (above),* as she looked at her launch into the Delaware River, December 5, 1931. She and her sistership, the *Washington,* soon to be launched, were not superliners in the class of the *Leviathan,* but up to that time they were the largest merchant ships yet built by the U.S. They filled a need for up-to-date, all-American ocean liners on the prestigious and highly competitive North Atlantic run. At launch, Mrs. Edith Kermit Roosevelt, widow of President Theodore Roosevelt, christened the ship by breaking across her bow a bottle containing waters gathered from all forty-eight states. [Built by New York Shipbuilding Company, Camden, New Jersey, 1932. 24,289 gross tons; 705 feet long; 86 feet wide. Steam turbines, twin screw. Service speed 20 knots. 1,239 passengers (582 cabin class, 461 tourist class, 196 third class).]

This aerial view *(opposite, top)* of the newly completed *Manhattan* shows the liner as she approaches New York harbor for the first time, on July 26, 1932. She had just completed highly successful trials off the Maine coast. The press expressed strong interest in the new ship, the first Atlantic luxury liner to be built in a U.S. shipyard in thirty-five years. The original squat stacks on the *Manhattan* as well as the *Washington* proved troublesome, mostly because they spread smoke and soot on the aft passenger decks. The stacks were soon heightened.

The ship's library had a comfortable Elizabethan decor *(opposite, bottom).*

Beginning in September 1939, to reinforce U.S. neutrality, the names of ships and shipping companies names were painted in large letters along the sides as well as on foredecks and on top decks. Re-creations of U.S. flags were also displayed on some vessels. Often, the names and colors were illuminated at night. American passenger ships continued commercial sailings well into 1940, long after European passenger ships had ceased service. Ships such as the *Washington*, shown (*opposite, top*) at her New York pier in October 1939, made special evacuation voyages out of Bordeaux, Genoa, and Lisbon. Thousands of anxious Americans, along with countless refugees, were clamoring to leave Europe. Helena Rubinstein, the cosmetics queen, and conductor Leopold Stokowski were among those who fled to the safe shores of America on board the *Washington* and the *Manhattan*.

This aerial view of the stern of the *Manhattan* (*opposite, bottom*) shows the liner arriving off New York, June 10, 1940, after an emergency evacuation voyage from Naples and Genoa.

In June 1941 the *Manhattan* and the *Washington* were refitted as the troop transports USS *Wakefield* and USS *Mount Vernon*. Onboard the *Wakefield*, as an example, her carrying capacity was greatly increased from 1,239 civilians to over 7,000 military personnel.

The *Manhattan*'s record in World War II was quite varied. In the spring of 1942 she sailed from New York to Colombo and Bombay, returning via Capetown. Next she sailed to the Clyde in Scotland via Halifax. But on the following voyage, in September 1942, she burned at sea off Halifax. At first thought to be a complete loss, she was towed to Nova Scotia and beached, but then was brought to the Boston Navy Yard for extensive repairs. In the restoration process an entire upper deck was removed, making her seem lower in profile. After being recommissioned in the spring of 1944, she made thirteen round trips to Liverpool with troops, followed by a voyage from Newport News to Gibraltar and Naples. In the spring of 1945 she sailed from Boston to Marseilles and Taranto, then on a voyage to Le Havre, Liverpool, and Antwerp, then on separate crossings to Le Havre, to Southampton, to Marseilles, and to Naples. In December 1945 she headed for the Pacific for the first time, departing Boston via Hampton Roads for the Panama Canal, Pearl Harbor, Taku, and finally Tsingtao in China. She returned to San Diego and then to San Pedro before heading west again to Guam and Kwajalein. In March 1946 she returned to San Pedro before a voyage to New York via the Panama Canal. On May 22, 1946, she was sent to the reserve fleet in the Hudson River. The former *Manhattan*, shown (*above*) against a setting sun in the North Atlantic on June 29, 1944, would never sail again. Sadly, her sailing career lasted but fourteen years, from 1932 until 1946, and only eight of them were in the commercial service for which she was intended.

The *Washington* was restored after the Second World War, but for austerity service carrying all-tourist-class passengers, 1,106 in all. She usually ran between New York, Southampton, Le Havre, and Bremerhaven with reduced fares. She is seen (*opposite, top*) at Le Havre in 1949. She was withdrawn in October 1951, just months before the United States Lines took delivery of the superliner *United States*, which set off on her Atlantic maiden voyage in July 1952. While used by the U.S. government's Military Sea Transportation Service for a time, the *Washington* soon joined her former sister in the mothball fleet in the Hudson River.

At its peak in the 1950s the Hudson River "reserve fleet" numbered some 200 ships. In this aerial photograph (*opposite, bottom*), a Liberty ship is being moved into position along one of the long rows of neatly nested vessels. They were positioned bow-in, bow-out for better stability. The fourth ship from the right end of the bottom row is the transport *Edmund B. Alexander*, the former *Amerika* of 1905. The third is the ex-liner *Manhattan*. The *Washington* was placed alongside her in February 1953.

By 1964 any future use for the former *Manhattan* or the *Washington* seemed remote. Greek shipowners, then interested in buying American passenger ships, might have had a look over them, but rethought their value considering the high costs of renewal and rebuilding against their ages. In July 1964 the *Wakefield*, the former *Manhattan*, was towed down the Hudson River, past the docks of New York City, and around to the former Federal Shipyard at Kearny, New Jersey, for scrapping. She is seen (*left*) sailing by the Tappan Zee Bridge.

EXCALIBUR. The Export Steamship Company, formed in 1919, was renamed the American Export Lines five years later and soon added passenger berths to some of its freighters. In 1930–31 the company ordered a quartet of combination passenger-cargo ships for its New York–Mediterranean service. Each was fitted with space for 125 passengers, all in splendid first-class quarters. Soon dubbed the "Four Aces," they were named *Excalibur* (commissioned in January 1931), *Exochorda, Exeter,* and *Excambion.* Immediately popular and successful, they were routed on forty-three-day round-trip voyages that sailed every other Tuesday afternoon from Jersey City to Ponta Delgada (Azores), Gibraltar, Marseilles, Naples, Alexandria, Jaffa, Haifa, Beirut, Alexandria, Piraeus, Naples, Leghorn, Genoa, Marseilles, Boston, and Jersey City. Fares were from $615 per person in a double on B Deck to $750 per person in a so-called Chambre de Luxe, a twin-bedded cabin with bedroom, sitting area, and full bath. In the summer of 1940 the *Excalibur (above)* took the Duke and Duchess of Windsor from the neutral port of Lisbon to the British island of Bermuda. The couple soon moved on to the Bahamas, where they remained until the war ended, in 1945. [Built by New York Shipbuilding Corporation, Camden, New Jersey, 1931. 9,359 gross tons; 474 feet long; 61 feet wide. Steam turbines, single screw. Service speed 16 knots. 125 all-first-class passengers.]

TARSUS. Three of the "Four Aces" were lost in the war, when they were U.S. Navy transports. The *Excalibur,* renamed USS *Joseph Hewes,* was torpedoed and sunk off Casablanca on November 11, 1942. The USS *Edward Rutledge,* the former *Exeter,* was sunk a day later, also off Casablanca. The USS *John Penn,* ex-*Excambion,* went to the bottom nine months later, on August 13, 1943, after being bombed by Japanese raiders off Guadalcanal. The *Exochorda,* renamed USS *Harry Lee,* was the only survivor. She was offered to American Export, who passed, then she was laid up until sold in 1948 to the Turkish Maritime Lines. Renamed *Tarsus,* she became the national flagship. Her accommodations were expanded to 465 passengers in three class-es, and she normally ran on Mediterranean service (mostly Istanbul to Piraeus, Naples, and Marseilles). *Tarsus* was also used for occasional cruises and "goodwill" voyages. She is seen (*opposite, top*) arriving at Miami on July 7, 1954, with a sign along her superstructure reading "Turkey Greets the United States." In 1960 she was chartered to the short-lived Fiesta Cruise Lines. Later that same year, on December 14, she was rammed by a burning Yugoslav tanker, the *Peter Zoranic,* in the Bosporus, then caught fire herself. She was gutted and had to be scrapped. [Built by New York Shipbuilding Corporation, Camden, New Jersey, 1931. 9,451 gross tons; 474 feet long; 61 feet wide. Steam turbines, single screw. Service speed 16 knots. 465 passengers (189 first class, 66 second class, 210 third class).]

SANTA PAULA (1932). The Grace Line had four superb sisterships, designed by the celebrated maritime architect William Francis Gibbs and built by the Federal Shipbuilding & Drydock Company at Kearny, New Jersey. The first of this twin-stack series was the *Santa Rosa,* launched in March 1932 and shown (*opposite, bottom*) in the lower right at the fitting-out berth. In the center of this photo, taken on June 11, 1932, is the *Santa Paula,* which has just gone down the ways. The *Santa Elena* and *Santa Lucia* are still under construction in adjoining slipways. Fitted with very fine accommodations, these ships were designed for extensive intercoastal service between New York and Seattle via the Caribbean, South America, the Panama Canal, Los Angeles, and San Francisco. But after a devastating West Coast maritime strike in 1934, the *Santa Lucia* was reassigned to the South American trade. By 1936 she had joined the other three sisters in full-time Caribbean service from New York. These seventeen-day round trips called at San Juan, Puerto Colombia, Cartagena, Aruba, Curaçao, La Guaira, Puerto Cabello, and back via San Juan and Nassau. [Built by Federal Shipbuilding & Drydock Company, Kearny, New Jersey, 1932. 9,135 gross tons; 508 feet long; 72 feet wide. Steam turbines, twin screw. Service speed 20 knots. 290 passengers (225 first class, 65 third class).]

SANTA ROSA (1932). These four Santa sisters became troopships in the Second World War. The *Santa Lucia*, renamed USS *Leedstown*, was sunk off Algiers on November 9, 1942. The *Santa Elena* was sunk almost a year later, on November 6, 1943, also off Algeria. The *Santa Rosa*, *(right)* arriving at New York on her first postwar commercial voyage in January 1947, and the *Santa Paula* were restored, to be used for twelve-day round-trip voyages that departed Grace Line's West 15th Street terminal at New York every Friday at noon for Aruba, La Guaira, Curaçao, and Cartagena. Minimum fare in the mid-1950s was $435. [Built by Federal Shipbuilding & Drydock Company, Kearny, New Jersey, 1932. 9,135 gross tons; 508 feet long; 72 feet wide. Steam turbines, twin screw. Service speed 20 knots. 225 all-first-class passengers after 1947.]

From 1958 to 1960 there were three ships afloat named *Santa Paula*. The confusing situation came about this way: In June 1958 a new *Santa Rosa* had come into service, running with the 1932-built *Santa Rosa*, which had been renamed *Santa Paula* to avoid confusion. The old *Santa Paula*, also of 1932 vintage, was then sent to the Bethlehem Steel shipyard in Hoboken and decommissioned. But in September a newly built *Santa Paula* came into service, and the other old *Santa Paula* was retired, also to Hoboken. Thus, two ships named *Santa Paula* sat nested together for two years. When the new *Santa Paula* put in at a nearby berth, the confusion was compounded.

The two older ships were finally sold in 1960 to Greek buyers, the Typaldos Lines, and were renamed: the *Santa Rosa* became the *Athinai*, the *Santa Paula*, the *Acropolis*. The latter is shown (*opposite, bottom*) with some boiler troubles, being towed out of New York harbor for Piraeus, Greece, in June 1961. The Greeks thoroughly refitted them: the *Athinai* offered accommodations in three classes—240 in first class, 180 in cabin class, and 200 in tourist class. She sailed mostly in the eastern Mediterranean, from Venice on fourteen-day round-trip voyages to Split, Piraeus, Limassol, Haifa, Larnaca, Rhodes, Piraeus, and back to Venice. The *Acropolis* was reconfigured with 450 all-one-class berths and usually served more as a cruise ship, traveling in the Mediterranean and to West Africa as well as to northern Europe—Norway (including remote Spitsbergen), the Baltic ports, and Iceland. Typaldos was bankrupt by 1967, however, and the two liners were laid up in Perama Bay, near Piraeus. The *Acropolis* was broken up in 1972–74, with the final pieces gone by 1977. For unexplained reasons the *Athinai* lasted another fifteen years. In 1978–79 she was used as a "floating prop" in the film *Raise the Titanic* and even had the name *Titanic* painted on her bow. Afterward, she returned to her lifeless moorings. In 1989, after a short tow, she was delivered to the scrappers at Aliaga in Turkey.

VERAGUA. Bananas were introduced to the American public in the 1870s, and by 1899 the United Fruit Company had become the biggest shipper of this popular item. Their fleet would soon consist of "banana boats" carrying up to 50,000 bunches of the fruit and as many as 100 passengers. The company's peak came in the early 1930s, when six "mail boats" of advanced design were ordered, three from the Newport News yard in Virginia and three from Bethlehem Steel in Massachusetts.

In a highly publicized, dual launching ceremony at Newport News, on August 15, 1931, Mrs. Herbert Hoover christened the first two of the United Fruit sisters, the *Talamanca* and the *Segovia* (renamed *Peten* after a subsequent fire at the yard while being fitted out). These ships were followed by the *Chiriqui*, *Antigua*, *Quirigua*, and finally the *Veragua*, shown (*above*) while sailing from New York on her maiden voyage on August 11, 1932. She was routed to Havana, Kingston, Cristóbal, and Puerto Limon. Three of the other sisters sailed from San Francisco to Central America, so travelers could go from the East Coast to the West Coast. All six "mail boats" survived World War II and were restored as passenger-cargo ships. Several went to the New Orleans-Caribbean-Central American trade, others revived the New York-Caribbean run. But increasing costs as well as competition from airlines finished off the New York trade by early 1953. Four of the ships, the *Quirigua*, the *Veragua*, the *Antigua*, and the *Talamanca*, were reduced to freighters. Four years later they were sold off to foreign-flag owners. The *Chiriqui* and the *Jamaica* ran United Fruit's last passenger ship service, from New Orleans, until March 1957. The company's last U.S.-flag freighter to carry a dozen passengers was sold to foreign interests in February 1971. [Built by Bethlehem Steel Company, Quincy, Massachusetts, 1932. 6,982 gross tons; 447 feet long; 60 feet wide. Steam turboelectric, twin screw. Service speed 18 knots. 100 one-class passengers as built.]

MORRO CASTLE. Along with the Grace Line's four sisters of the *Santa Rosa* class, the Ward Line's *Morro Castle* and *Oriente* were among the finest U.S.-flag liners built for Caribbean service. The two latter ships were used in a weekly service between New York and Havana. The *Morro Castle* in particular was said to be the last word in American ship construction and in maritime safety standards. She is seen here *(left)*, on March 6, 1930, about to be launched. [Built by Newport News Shipbuilding & Drydock Company, Newport News, Virginia, 1930. 11,520 gross tons; 508 feet long; 71 feet wide. Steam turbo-electric, twin screw. Service speed 20 knots. 530 passengers (430 first class, 100 tourist class).]

On her normal northbound run from Havana to New York, tragedy struck the *Morro Castle* as she steamed along the New Jersey coastline in rain and rough seas on the night of September 8, 1934. Just before the gala farewell dinner, the captain was found dead in his stateroom. Hours later, fire was discovered in a locker off the writing room, but its extent was minimized and no distress calls were sent. Unfortunately, the ship's firefighting equipment was in poor condition, and the crew lacked discipline and necessary training. Around three in the morning a distress call was sent, but inexperienced Coast Guard officers on the all-night watch did not follow through properly. The ship was now drifting toward the beach as attempts were made to lower the lifeboats. Further chaos and disorganization ensued. One seventy-person lifeboat departed with eight people aboard, six of whom were crew. Of the first eighty in other lifeboats, all but seven were members of the crew. By 4:30 A.M., passenger ships such as the *Monarch of Bermuda* had answered the distress calls from the *Morro Castle*, which was engulfed in flames *(opposite, top)*. Local fishing boats came to assist as well. In all, 162 passengers and crew were rescued. A towline was attached to the blistering liner, but it soon snapped and the ship drifted on to the Asbury Park beach.

By Sunday morning, September 10, an estimated 25,000 people had gathered along the beach and on the boardwalk to view the smoldering wreck *(opposite, middle)*. Of the 316 passengers and 230 crew on board, 91 passengers and 31 crew members perished.

In the initial hearings on the disaster, life-saving equipment deficiencies, poor condition of the lifeboats, and lack of rigid fire and lifeboat drills were all found to be at fault. The acting captain and chief engineer were given prison sentences, which were later appealed. Later evidence suggested that the blaze was started deliberately by Chief Radio Officer George Rogers, who, it was uncovered, had a history of setting fires. He was later convicted in an unrelated murder case and died in prison in 1958.

The $4 million *Morro Castle* was scrapped for less than $100,000 at Baltimore. She is seen in this June 11, 1935 photo *(opposite, bottom)* with funnels, upper decks, and aft mast removed. Her tragedy brought to light lax enforcement of U.S. safety regulations.

ORIENTE. The *Morro Castle's* twin sister, the *Oriente*, shown (*above*) here arriving at her East River berth on September 22, 1939, carried on the New York-Havana service single-handedly. She would leave from the foot of Wall Street on Tuesday afternoons at four o'clock, arrive at Havana on Saturday at eight in the morning, and remain in port overnight. Minimum fare in the late 1930s was $65; a suite cost $150 per person.

The *Oriente* was taken over by the U.S. Navy in June 1941 and restyled as the troopship USS *Thomas H. Barry*. Her capacity was officially 3,609 troops, and wartime voyages took her out of New York as well as Boston and New Orleans to the Caribbean, the South Pacific, Morocco, and Australia. In July 1943 she began the first of twenty-three Atlantic crossings. In January 1946 she was converted to carry military dependents, 390 adults and 148 children. Laid up afterward, she was declared surplus in 1957 and that November was handed over to Baltimore breakers, almost at the same location where her sister had been demolished twenty-two years earlier. [Built by Newport News Shipbuilding & Drydock Company, Newport News, Virginia, 1930. 11,520 gross tons; 508 feet long; 71 feet wide. Steam turboelectric, twin screw. Service speed 20 knots. 530 passengers (430 first class, 100 tourist class).]

PRESIDENT COOLIDGE. Two of the finest liners ever to sail the Pacific were the Dollar Line sisterships *President Hoover* and *President Coolidge*, which were launched in December 1930 and in February 1931, respectively. Big, powerful, and luxurious ships, they were the American response to new tonnage just arrived on the transpacific route, namely Canadian Pacific's *Empress of Japan* and three new Japanese ships. The *Hoover* and the *Coolidge* were, in fact, the first passenger ships to be designed from the keel upward for Dollar, as all their previous passenger ships had been built as troop transports and later converted to accommodate passengers.

The *President Coolidge* departed on October 22 for a gala maiden cruise from New York to Havana, the Panama Canal, Acapulco, Los Angeles, San Francisco, Honolulu, Yokohama, Kobe, Hong Kong, Manila, and Shanghai. Afterward she was based on the West Coast. The twenty-four-day voyage from San Francisco to Shanghai was priced at $331 in first class in 1937.

Both ships had eventful careers. The *President Hoover* was attacked by Chinese planes in the Whampoo River in August 1935. The *Coolidge* rammed and sank the tanker *Frank H. Buck* near San Francisco's Golden Gate on March 6, 1937. That December, the *President Hoover* ran aground on a volcanic island on the southern tip of Taiwan. The passengers were soon transferred to Hoishoto Island and then taken to Manila. Salvage vessels attempted to free the *Hoover* despite continuous storms and rough seas. After two weeks, however, she was reported to be cracked amidships, listing twenty degrees, and in danger of breaking in half. Dollar released the wreckage to Japanese scrappers. Another serious loss was the *President Coolidge*, the company's largest and finest liner. On October 26, 1942, with 5,100 troops and crew on board, approaching the harbor of Espiritu Santo in the New Hebrides, she sailed into a mine-filled channel. After the first explosion the ship's master ordered a full astern, but her own momentum thrust her into two additional mines. She sank in deep water, but fortunately a disciplined evacuation resulted in the loss of only two of the 5,100 aboard. The caption of this wartime news photo (*opposite, top*) read, "Her decks empty of men, her lifeboat davits empty of boats, a wisp of smoke curling from a funnel, the *President Coolidge* slides under the water of a South Pacific island harbor, victim of a mine." [Built by Newport News Shipbuilding & Drydock Company, Newport News, Virginia, 1931. 21,936 gross tons; 654 feet long; 81 feet wide. Steam turboelectric, twin screw. Service speed 21 knots. 650 passengers (340 first class, 150 tourist, 160 Asiatic steerage).]

MARIPOSA (1931). The great success of the *Malolo* of 1927 led the Matson Navigation Company of San Francisco to build not just a new, even larger liner for the San Francisco-Los Angeles-Honolulu service, but two additional luxury ships to be used on the South Pacific and Australia route. These three ships proved to be among the largest, finest, and most enduring liners of all time. In the Pacific in the 1930s they were without serious rivals. They were named *Mariposa*, seen *(below, left)* in Pago Pago harbor on May 26, 1937, *Monterey*, and *Lurline*.

Ordered from the Bethlehem Steel Company's Quincy, Massachusetts, yard, the *Mariposa* was launched in July 1931 and placed in service in the following January. The *Monterey* went down the ways in October 1931 and was commissioned in May 1932. Both of these ships, while operating under the Matson Line banner, were officially owned by a subsidiary, Oceanic Steamship Company, which had its interests in the southern Pacific. Their general routing was from San Francisco and Los Angeles to Honolulu, Pago Pago, Suva, Auckland, Sydney, Melbourne, and then return via the same ports. The last of this splendid threesome, the *Lurline*, was launched in July 1932 and entered service in

January 1933. She was paired with the overbooked *Malolo* on the Honolulu service. [Built by Bethlehem Steel Company, Quincy, Massachusetts, 1931. 18,017 gross tons; 632 feet long; 79 feet wide. Steam turbines, twin screw. Service speed 20 knots. 704 passengers (475 first class, 229 cabin class).]

On board the *Lurline* the elegant main lounge *(below, right)* was unusually large, and the main restaurant was decorated in brilliant murals of bygone clipper ships and palm-fringed isles. The smoking room included a bar at one end. Other facilities included a gentlemen's club room, a library, verandah café, gymnasium, two large swimming pools, and playrooms for the younger guests. The restaurants had air conditioning, then a great attraction for passenger ships, and the system regulated temperature as well as humidity. Every first-class stateroom included wardrobes, dressing tables, Thermos bottles filled with ice water, electric fans, extra baggage space, a telephone, and private bath. The five-day voyage from San Francisco to Honolulu in 1935 was priced from $125 in first class and $85 in cabin. San Francisco to Sydney, a twenty-day trip, was $367 in first class and $246 in cabin class.

MONTEREY (1932). A Los Angeles newspaper caption for this photo *(opposite, top)*, dated June 1, 1932, read, "$15 Million Worth of Ships!" The brand-new *Monterey* is here being prepared for her maiden voyage to South Pacific waters, with her predecessor, the *Malolo*, berthed just behind. The *Monterey* (and *Mariposa*), while belonging to Oceanic Steamship Company, an arm of Matson, had blue and buff funnels; the *Malolo* and the *Lurline*, both on the Hawaiian service for Matson directly, had the addition of large blue "M's" on their stacks. [Built by Bethlehem Steel Company, Quincy, Massachusetts, 1932. 18,017 gross tons; 632 feet long; 79 feet wide. Steam turbines, twin screw. Service speed 20 knots. 701 passengers (472 first class, 229 cabin class).]

Each of the four big Matson liners served as troopships during the Second World War. On January 10, 1944, the gray-painted, cannon-equipped *Monterey* *(opposite, bottom)* is docked stern-first in the floating dock at Bethlehem Steel's 56th Street yard in Brooklyn. She is undergoing much-needed repairs, having been in military service for two years. With her troop capacity listed as 4,296, but often

exceeded, she had been sailing to the South Pacific and Australia, and on the Atlantic to Casablanca, Liverpool, Gourock (Scotland), and Marseilles. She had also visited Pearl Harbor, Manila, and numerous small Pacific islands.

LURLINE. It had been Matson's intention to revive the three larger sisters after the war, but shipyard and refit costs had just about tripled. The projects for the *Mariposa* and *Monterey* were put aside; the *Lurline* was refitted at the Union Engineering Shipyards at Alameda *(above)*, just across the bay from San Francisco. She had cost $7.9 million to build in 1933; her two-year restoration in 1946–48 cost $19 million. She returned to the Honolulu service that April, replacing the *Matsonia* (ex-*Malolo*). That ship, which had been only provisionally restored, was then sold off to the Panamanian-flag Home Lines to become their *Atlantic*. [Built by Bethlehem Steel Company, Quincy, Massachusetts, 1932. 18,564 gross tons (1948); 631 feet long; 79 feet wide. Steam turbines, twin screw. 761 all-first-class passengers.]

The *Lurline* and the American President Lines' *President Cleveland* and *President Wilson* were the largest U.S.-flag liners operating from the West Coast in the late 1940s. The all-white Matson ship is seen (*above*) being overhauled at Bethlehem Steel's San Francisco shipyard. Sixty-one feet of anchor chain reached the drydock floor below, attached to an anchor weighing seven tons.

The arrival of a Matson liner off Honolulu was a major event, known locally as 'Boat Day.' Tradition called for a welcoming escort of outrigger canoes. This publicity photo (**top**) shows a crowd greeting the inbound *Lurline* in the mid-1950s.

The *Mariposa* and *Monterey* were laid up in 1947 at Alameda, California. Their futures seemed uncertain, although Matson hoped to restore at least one of them. In December 1953, the *Mariposa* was sold to the Panama-registered Home Lines and sent to an Italian shipyard to be refitted as the *Homeric*. Thereafter she made Atlantic crossings between northern Europe and Canada for about eight months of the year, then Caribbean cruises from New York in winter. Damaged by fire off New Jersey on July 1, 1973, she was laid up for a time before being sold early the next year to Taiwanese scrappers.

The *Monterey* was revived by Matson in 1956–57, as the *Matsonia*. She left Alameda under tow on March 15, 1956, and reached the Panama Canal on April 7. With a crew of twenty-five, she changed tugs, to the *Christine Moran* and *M. Moran* as shown (**middle**) for the remaining tow to the Newport News shipyard in Virginia, which she reached on April 20. In this view the ship is forty miles east of Jacksonville, Florida, being towed at about 7.5 knots. Her reconstruction cost $17.5 million.

MATSONIA. Recommissioned in May 1957, the *Matsonia* (**bottom**) then took up her role on the Honolulu service together with the *Lurline*. Six years later, in the face of airline competition and rising costs, the *Lurline* was sold. The *Matsonia* soon took over her running-mate's more popular name. The original *Lurline* was sold to the Chandris Lines in September 1963 and restyled as the all-tourist-class *Ellinis* for Australian immigrant and around-the-world economy voyages. Her capacity was increased from 760 to 1,642. Turbine parts were taken from the laid-up *Homeric*, the former *Mariposa*, in 1973 and installed aboard the ex-*Lurline*. The *Ellinis* was laid up in 1980 and then scrapped on Taiwan seven years later. The last *Lurline* (ex-*Monterey*, ex-*Matsonia*), which ended Matson's Honolulu service in 1970, was also sold to the Chandris Lines and was rebuilt as the *Britanis*. She too then worked the around-the-world service as well as running on a number of cruises. Retired from commercial service in 1995, she did a stint as a refugee accommodation center in Cuba before being laid up in Tampa. In 1998 she was sold to intermediary buyers and renamed *Belophin I* in preparation for scrapping in India. In December 1998 she was reportedly resold for use as a floating hotel at San Francisco under the name *Normandie*. Sold finally to Middle Eastern scrappers, she sank while empty and under tow off South Africa in October 2000.

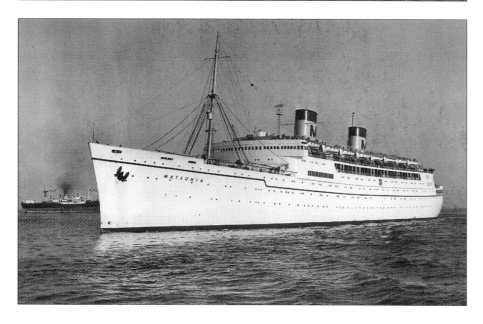

CHAPTER 7

New National Flagship: *America*

The great ship *America*, 33,500 tons and over 700 feet long, was the start of the largest shipbuilding program the world has ever seen. The Merchant Marine Act of 1936 was enacted into law because of the U.S. government's decision to strengthen the American fleet. War seemed increasingly likely in Europe, and President Franklin D. Roosevelt convinced the Congress that the U.S. had to be ready to defend itself at sea. In all, some 6,000 merchant ships were built in the U.S. between the launching of the *America* in 1937 and the completion of the *United States* some fifteen years later.

Beginning in 1938 most of the construction program was under the overall supervision of the U.S. Maritime Commission. At that time there were about a dozen shipyards in the U.S. capable of building big, deep-sea vessels. By 1943 there were over eighty shipbuilding plants on all four coasts. By the time the big program ended, 45 percent of the commission's ships had been built on the West Coast, 34 percent on the East Coast, 19 percent on the Gulf Coast, and 2 percent on the Great Lakes. They were all needed as the war effort went into high gear. The commission started with a goal of fifty ships a year. This figure then doubled annually, so that by 1942 it was up to 800. The rate of growth slowed in 1943, when about 1,000 ships were launched. In 1942-43 alone, some 18 million tons of merchant mariners were produced. This figure included all types of vessels, even tugboats, but was dominated by about 2,800 Liberty ships, 500 Victory ships, and 500 tankers. And the *America* was Hull number 1. She was the nation's largest, fastest, finest liner. Renamed USS *West Point*, she was an active troopship in worldwide service.

"The 1940s turned into a frenzy of building," noted Jack Weatherford. "America became obsessed with the production of everything: arms, ships, planes, uniforms. The reasoning was that overproduction would help defeat the enemy. Many people think this is how we won the war—the constant supplies of war equipment from the factories and the shipyards."

The *America* was refitted for commercial passenger service in 1946. As the flagship of the largest merchant fleet of all time, she was one of the most popular ships in the immediate postwar era. Transatlantic travel resumed, and more than a decade would pass before the airlines would come to dominate that segment of the travel market. The *America* was in the medium-sized class, along with such ships as Holland America's *Nieuw Amsterdam*, Cunard's *Mauretania*, and the French Line's *Ile de France*. But, of course, the *America* was a prelude to the *United States*, almost a test run for what was surely the most advanced passenger liner of her time. This big new ship was a blazing success, overshadowing her smaller, slower running-mate. But the *America* did not fade away. In fact, she was preferred by travelers who wanted a somewhat longer voyage or who found her decor and overall ambience cozier and more intimate than that aboard the bigger ship.

In the early 1960s the *America* was the first big American passenger ship to be retired. Her layup marked the beginning of the end for all the grand postwar transatlantic liners, even the mighty *United States*. The *America* soon went on to a new life with Greek owners, sailing in around-the-world service as the *Australis*. Several names and decades later, in 1994, she was wrecked in the Canary Islands. Her last remnants were still clinging to the rugged coastline there as this book went to press.

AMERICA. The late 1930s was a time when more medium-sized liners were built for the North Atlantic trade. The Netherlands, for example, introduced the 36,000-ton *Nieuw Amsterdam* in 1938, and Britain's Cunard Line added the *Mauretania* (35,000 tons) the following year. The United States Lines needed a third liner to maintain a weekly service with the sisters *Manhattan* and *Washington,* but had no interest in replacing the money-losing superliner *Leviathan* (laid up in 1934 and scrapped four years later) with another huge ship. They did, however, want a larger version of the 24,000-ton *Manhattan* and her sister, so they ordered the 34,000-ton *America* in 1937. The first keel plate was laid at Newport News in August 1938, and on August 31, 1939, the largest liner yet built in the United States was appropriately named by the nation's First Lady, Mrs. Eleanor Roosevelt *(above).* The cheers and the joys were muted a day later, when Hitler's forces made their peace-shattering invasion into Poland. As crews worked feverishly toward the *America's* summer 1940 delivery, her owners realized that any European passenger service was now out of the question. [Built by Newport News Shipbuilding & Drydock Company, Newport News, Virginia, 1940. 33,961 gross tons; 723 feet long; 94 feet wide. Steam turbines, twin screw. Service speed 22.5 knots. 1,046 passengers (516 first class, 371 cabin class, 159 tourist class).]

Soon after the *America* went down the ways on that summer afternoon in August 1939 *(below),* her brilliant designer, William Francis Gibbs, began sketches and preliminary lists for a larger, far more powerful vessel of similar design. He thought of specifications of over 800 feet and as much as 40,000 tons. But World War II pushed much of this aside—at least until 1943, when planning resumed in earnest. The ship that emerged nearly a decade later, in 1952, was the extraordinary *United States,* the fastest liner ever built. While smaller and slower, the *America* was her forerunner in many ways, the test case.

Although Gibbs loved big, impressive funnels, he had used small, squat stacks on the *Manhattan* and the *Washington* and, later, on the *America*. But all these sets were failures, spreading smoke and soot on the aft passenger decks. Soon after completion the funnels had to be raised in height. In this view of the *America* (*above*), dated April 1940, the original short stacks are in place.

When the *America* steamed into New York harbor for the first time, in July 1940, she was given a rousing welcome (*opposite, top*). Typically, she wore the "neutrality markings" that had been placed on all U.S.-flag and other neutral ships of the time. She was a strikingly handsome ship, her looks enhanced by the taller funnels. The forward stack was a "dummy," installed just for effect and added ventilation.

United States Lines did actually think of laying up their brand-new flagship as she came out of the Newport News yard. Instead, they used the ship in temporary cruise service, sailing to the Caribbean and on inter-coastal voyages to California from New York. She is seen in her first commercial departure (*opposite, bottom*), sailing from New York's Pier 61 at the foot of West 21st Street, August 10, 1940. Within a year the *America* would be called to more urgent duty: war service as a large troop transport.

The wartime *America* was repainted all in gray and renamed the USS *West Point*. (The old *America* of 1905 was also on duty, but as the troopship USS *Edmund B. Alexander*.) The *West Point's* carrying capacity was officially listed at 8,175, but there are records of the big ex-liner carrying over 9,000 military personnel. This photograph (*above*) was taken of the jam-packed ship as thousands cheered the G.I.s' return from duty overseas to New York's Pier 86 in August 1945. Throughout the war the *West Point* maintained a busy sailing schedule, her total mileage the equivalent of about fifteen circumnavigations. She called at ports around the world, from India and Australia to South Africa and, of course, Europe, passing through the Panama and Suez canals. During this time she had experienced a few close calls. Off Singapore Japanese bombers came within about fifty yards of the anchored liner. Nazi torpedoes crossed her bow off Brazil, and enemy bombers just missed her in the Red Sea, at Port Suez, and off Australia.

It cost about $6 million to restore the *America* in 1946. The results produced one of the most striking contemporary maritime decors, the first-class ballroom (*below*).

The *America* was acknowledged to be one of the most beautiful Atlantic liners of the late 1940s and 50s. She had luxury blended with coziness, and was noted for her fine service and kitchens. The first-class main lounge *(above)* was an impressive two-deck space. The big ship crossed regularly between New York, Cobh, Le Havre, and Southampton (later extended to Bremerhaven, West Germany). She did only very occasional cruises, down to Bermuda, Nassau, and the Caribbean, and for a short time, in the late 40s, her hull was experimentally repainted in gray as a form of heat resistance.

This first-class stateroom, number U-59 *(below),* consisted of a sitting area placed between the two single beds, with double portholes and a desk unit on the far right. The room also included full facilities: bath, shower, and toilet. This room was priced at $415 per person in the early 1950s for the six-day passage to Southampton or Le Havre.

The *America* was often included in the gatherings, the so-called stack-ups, of liners along New York City's West Side piers. Known as Luxury Liner Row and often photographed for newspaper centerfolds, these piers went from Number 84, at West 44th Street (at the bottom of this aerial view), to Pier 97, at 57th Street (not shown here). In the scene (*above*) dated September 26, 1956, from top to bottom are the *Mauretania*, *Queen Elizabeth*, and the freighter *Alsatia*, all Cunard; the *United States* and the *America*; and finally the *Cristoforo Colombo*, Italian Line. With four Moran tugs along her starboard side, it is clear that the *America* has just made an early-afternoon arrival from Europe—as opposed to her customary arrivals at eight o'clock in the morning.

After 1952 the *America*, seen in this early photo taken from her bridge (*opposite, top*) acted as consort to the record-breaking *United States*. Actually, some travelers preferred her to the new flagship because of her less hurried pace and added time at sea. Like all the great Atlantic liners, the *America* encountered her share of rough weather. In this view (*opposite, bottom*), dating from September 1948, a huge wave engulfs the very front of her bow.

In the early 1960s the *America* began to make cruises from New York to such warm-weather ports as Bermuda, Nassau, San Juan, and St. Thomas. A five-day holiday cruise to Bermuda was priced from $145 in 1961. The Atlantic trade to and from Europe was already in deepening decline. The first transatlantic jet service began in October 1958, and within a year the airlines had two-thirds of all traffic, then a crushing 95 percent by 1965. While United States Lines' directors had once talked of building a new liner, perhaps even another superliner, to sail with the *United States* and replace the *America*, the idea never came to pass. The aging *America* was already losing too much money. A determining blow occurred in September 1963, when a labor dispute among her crew forced cancellation of a sailing just hours before her departure for Europe. With no hope of a quick resolution, the *America's* future sailings were canceled, and the ship moved across the Hudson to a Hoboken shipyard to what became a five-month layup.

Resuming her posted schedules in February, 1964, she carried fewer and fewer passengers. In October she completed her last crossing for the United States Lines. She was sold soon afterward for $1.5 million to the Chandris Lines, who refitted her as the all-tourist class *Australis*. Her capacity was more than doubled, to 2,258, which included the addition of six-berth cabins. She was thereafter employed on three-month trips around the world, beginning at Southampton, England, and always including ports in Australia and New Zealand to land immigrants. But then even this trade faded because of jetliner competition. The *Australis* made her last run in November 1978.

In a misguided move the following spring, the great ship was sent to New York, renamed *America*, and scheduled by the short-lived Venture Cruise Lines for a series of inexpensive short cruises. The first two sailings were marred by scandalous conditions: unworkable toilets, food shortages, even talk of rats. She was quickly pulled from service and then, in a strange twist, resold to Chandris. The liner was brought back to Greece, refitted (her forward, dummy stack was removed), and renamed *Italis* for Mediterranean cruises. But she was laid up that autumn, too old, too expensive, unable to secure further charters for cruising. Though she lived on in the hearts of thousands of transatlantic passengers, who remembered the sight of the mighty ship at her New York pier (*above*), her sailing days were over.

While laid up at a vast anchorage of other out-of-work ships in Perama Bay, not far from Piraeus in Greece, the rusting *Italis* passed to other owners. She became the *Alferdoss*, then the *Noga*, and finally the *American Star*. Over the years there were rumors

that she would become a floating hotel in West Africa, a prison in Texas, a yacht marina at Montreal, a hotel at New York, a floating trade fair for the Chinese, a reactivated cruise ship. Renamed *American Star* by new owners in 1993, she was slated to become an ocean-liner hotel moored near Bangkok. Some tugs were hired for the long tow out to the Far East, but Suez Canal authorities refused permission for her transit. They feared an accident with the old vessel. In January 1994 an oceangoing tug guided her out through the Mediterranean and the Straits of Gibraltar for the tow around Africa and across the Indian Ocean. But she soon met her end. In ferocious, hurricane winds the towlines snapped and the ship slammed ashore on a remote northern part of the Canary Islands. The four crewmen aboard were rescued by helicopter. In this view (*below*), dating from August 1997, only about 400 feet of the liner remained. While some artifacts had been removed by locals, scrapping was not only expensive, but it was also dangerous. Recent reports have suggested that this leftover half might become free and then sink, a sad end for the splendid former *America*.

CHAPTER 8
"Combo" Ships: Passengers and Cargo

"The 'combo' ship was perfected by Americans," according to Frank Braynard. "They used high standards plus novelty. The 'Four Aces' of American Export Lines were great examples. Just calling them the 'Four Aces' was a wonderful stroke of marketing. The name was invented by Al Graham, the public relations officer for American Export. They had all-first-class quarters of the highest postwar standard, and they were unique in being the first fully air conditioned passenger ships. In fact, I think the 'Aces' were the most successful of all U.S.-built combination passenger-cargo vessels."

The concept of the modern combination ship was not born during World War II. It had first blossomed during the interwar period. There were the first 'Four Aces,' launched in 1931, and such ships as Holland America Line's *Noordam* and *Zaandam* of 1938, each of which carried 150 passengers in luxurious, one-class accommodations in addition to considerable cargo. The idea captured the imagination of more and more U.S. shipowners. In 1939, for example, the Panama Line built three splendid ships, the *Panama*, the *Ancon*, and the *Cristóbal*, which could carry just over 200 passengers each, along with cargo. Their interiors as well their exteriors were stunning examples of Art Deco excellence. "They were magnificent ships in every way," noted Braynard. "Even when they were scrapped, decades later, they looked sleek and modern. They were the creations of naval architect George Sharp, a native of Scotland who had served as a young assistant on the liners *Dakota* and *Minnesota* when they were built in 1905."

Other shipping lines soon turned to the "combo" concept. Delta, Farrell, American, and Grace took delivery of some vessels of this type before the war. Other lines, such as American Merchant and Moore McCormack, saw their orders shuffled aside in the wake of war-related construction. Inevitably, over time the combinations fell out of favor. By the 1960s the blend of passengers and freight became less and less profitable. One problem was that schedules had to take into consideration both sides of the combination. Sometimes passengers had to wait for late cargo, other times late-delivered freight was left behind in order to keep posted, passenger-oriented departures. Some ships, like the Grace Line's *Santa Isabel* and her sisters, worked on forty-two-day cycles, while others, such as the *President Monroe* and the *President Polk*, sailed around the world on ninety-five-day itineraries. By 1970 just about all these ships were gone, replaced by a new generation of faster, more efficient, but decidedly less elegant container-cargo vessels. Aficionados of this type of travel booked on old-fashioned freighters with accommodations for a dozen or so passengers.

ANCON. On the eve of the Second World War the U.S. government-owned Panama Railroad Company contracted with Bethlehem Steel's Quincy, Massachusetts, yard for the construction of three fine new sisterships—the *Panama*, the *Ancon*, shown *(top)* just prior to launching on September 30, 1939, and the *Cristóbal*. Handsome-looking combination ships, they were designed especially for the vital passenger, mail, and cargo links between the United States and the Panama Canal Zone, running between New York and Cristóbal. Their light-gray hulls were balanced by white superstructures, silver masts and booms, and a large buff-colored single stack. [Built by Bethlehem Steel Company, Quincy, Massachusetts, 1939. 9,978 gross tons; 493 feet long; 64 feet wide. Steam turbines, twin screw. Service speed 17.5 knots. 216 all-first-class passengers.]

CRISTÓBAL. These three Panama Line ships were said to be among the very finest American combo ships. Their interiors were done by Raymond Loewy, often called "the king of streamline." He had already designed Pennsylvania Railroad trains, Hoover vacuum cleaners, Proctor steam irons, and much else. Internally, the ships were fine examples of high Art Deco—stainless steel trims, tubular chairs, and number-less clocks. All state-rooms had private bath, and some included the novelty of shared, glass-enclosed verandahs. Some of the public rooms were two decks high, and the dining room was air conditioned, an attractive feature for such tropic-bound ships. Spanking new, the *Cristóbal* *(bottom)* rests in the floating dock at Bethlehem Steel's East Boston repair yard prior to delivery to her owners. It is July 1939, and she is being given final touches prior to the handing over and her maiden voyage from New York. [Built by Bethlehem Steel Company, Quincy, Massachusetts, 1939. 9,978 gross tons; 493 feet long; 64 feet wide. Steam turbines, twin screw. Service speed 17.5 knots. 216 all-first class passengers.]

The three sisters served with distinction in the Second World War. The *Ancon*, shown (**left**) in September 1945, was refitted by the U.S. Navy as a communications center and an accommodation ship for the commanders of amphibious operations. She served in the assault on Sicily and in the Normandy invasion, then in the Pacific at the Okinawa landings. In August 1945, moored in Tokyo Bay, the *Ancon* told the world of the Japanese surrender. The ships resumed sailing to the Caribbean after the war. In 1957 the *Panama* was sold to American President Lines and began sailing as their *President Hoover*, based at San Francisco for sailings to Hawaii and the Far East. She was sold to the Chandris Lines in 1964, who restyled her as the Mediterranean cruise ship *Regina* (later *Regina Prima*). After a long layup she was broken up in Turkey in 1985. The *Ancon* sailed from New York until 1961, when she was sold to the Maine Maritime Academy. As the *State of Maine* she was used as the cadet training ship until broken up in 1973. The *Cristóbal* continued sailing for the Panama Line, but from New Orleans and in "official only" service with twelve passenger berths. She was withdrawn in 1981 and then dismantled.

DELBRASIL. The New Orleans-based Delta Line, the Mississippi Shipping Company, ordered six combo ships for their service to the east coast of South America—Rio de Janeiro, Santos, Montevideo, and Buenos Aires—in 1938. The first three, *Delbrasil*, shown (**below**) being launched on December 16, 1939, *Delorleans*, and *Delargentino*, were designed to carry sixty-seven passengers in luxurious accommodations. The *Delbrasil* soon afterward was, like her sisters, called to more urgent duty. She became the U.S. Navy transport USS *George F. Elliott*, then was sold in 1948 to the Farrell Lines, who renamed her *African Endeavor*. The *Delorleans* became the USS *Crescent City* and later served as the *Golden Bear*, a training ship for the California Maritime Academy. As of 1999 she was in layup near San Francisco. The *Delargentino*, which became the USS *J. W. McAndrew*, later sailed as the *African Enterprise* for the Farrell Lines. The remaining trio, the *Deluruguay*, *Delorleans II*, and the *Delargentino II*, were requisitioned by the U.S. Navy during construction and were finished as the transports USS *Charles Carroll*, USS *Calvert*, and USS *Monrovia*. [*Delbrasil*: Built by Bethlehem Steel Company, Sparrows Point, Maryland, 1940. 7,997 gross tons; 491 feet long; 66 feet wide. Steam turbines, single screw. Service speed 16.5 knots. 67 all-first-class passengers.]

AFRICAN ENDEAVOR. The New York-headquartered Farrell Lines operated a sizable fleet of twelve-passenger freighters and two combo liners, the eighty-two-passenger *African Endeavor,* (**above**), shown in Table Bay, Capetown, and the *African Enterprise.* They were originally built for the Delta Line and then converted for use as Navy transports in the 1940s. With their appearances enhanced by the fitting of tapered funnels, they were refitted for Farrell in 1949. Like large "yachts," they were used on fifty-six-day round-trip voyages between the United States and Africa, sailing from New York City (Farrell's terminal was then at the foot of 33rd Street in Brooklyn) to Capetown, Port Elizabeth, Durban, South Africa, and Lourenco Marques (Maputo) with a turnaround at Beira, then in Portuguese East Africa. For businessmen the voyage from New York to Capetown was advertised as "sixteen days direct." [Built by Bethlehem Steel Company, Sparrows Point, Maryland, 1940. 7,997 gross tons; 491 feet long; 66 feet wide. Steam turbines, single screw. Service speed 16.5 knots. 82 all-first class passengers.]

The dining rooms on board the *African Enterprise* (**right**) and the *African Endeavor* were highlighted by South African artwork. Other public rooms included a lounge and a smoking room. The passenger loads often numbered fifty and sometimes as few as twenty-five, and consequently there was the mood of a large yacht. But these ships were expensive to operate, and their unique passenger service to and from Africa had rather limited appeal. Within a decade, by 1959, the two sisters were withdrawn and laid up in the James River reserve fleet in Virginia. A decade later, in 1969, they were sold to scrappers at Baltimore.

PRESIDENT POLK. For its ninety-five-day around-the-world service American President Lines ordered six combo liners in 1939–40: *President Jackson, President Monroe, President Hayes, President Garfield, President Van Buren,* and *President Polk,* shown (*above*) passing under the San Francisco–Oakland Bay Bridge. All six were soon called to wartime service and, by 1946, only the *Monroe* and *Polk* were returned to commercial service. The other four became permanent Navy transports, the last surviving of which, the USS *President Hayes,* was demolished in 1975. [*President Polk:* Built by Newport News Shipbuilding & Drydock Company, Newport News, Virginia, 1940. 9,225 gross tons; 492 feet long; 70 feet wide. Steam turbines, single screw. Service speed 16.5 knots. 96 all-first-class passengers.]

Passengers aboard the *President Monroe* and the *President Polk* often made the entire three-month circumnavigation. The routing was from New York (the American President terminal at Pier 9, Jersey City) to Cristóbal, Balboa, Acapulco, Los Angeles, San Francisco, Honolulu, Yokohama, Kobe, Hong Kong, Saigon, Singapore, Penang, then around the southern tip of India to Cochin, Bombay, Karachi, Port Suez, Port Said, Alexandria, Naples, Marseilles, Genoa, and Leghorn before returning to the United States. Between voyages these ships also did so-called "coastal swings" to load additional cargo, calling at Boston, Philadelphia, Baltimore, and Norfolk/Hampton Roads. Minimum fare in the early 1960s for the complete world voyage was $2,990. Public accommodations on the *President Monroe* included a main lounge (*below*) with a wood-burning fireplace, an outdoor pool, all cabins with private bathrooms, and partial air conditioning.

Withdrawn in 1965, these two ships were replaced by luxurious freighters with a dozen passenger berths. The *President Monroe* was sold to Greek buyers and became the *Marianna VI,* while the *President Polk* became the South American "cattle boat" *Gaucho Martin Fierro* and later the Greek-flag *Minotaurus.*

DEL MAR. After the war, in 1946–47, the Delta Line added three fine combo ships for its New Orleans–South America service. They had gleaming contemporary interiors and were among the first commercial ships equipped with an added navigational aid: radar. The *Del Mar*—shown *(above)* being readied for launch on May 17, 1946—the *Del Norte*, and the *Del Sud* worked forty-four-day round-trip itineraries, priced from $810 (or $19 per person per day) in the early 1960s. They were routed from New Orleans and Houston to St. Thomas, Rio de Janeiro, Santos, and Buenos Aires, returning via Santos, Rio, and Curaçao. In 1967 they were downgraded to twelve-passenger freighters, and in 1972, against old age and rising operational costs, were sold to scrap merchants in Taiwan. [Built by Ingalls Shipbuilding Corporation, Pascagoula, Mississippi, 1946. 10,073 gross tons; 495 feet long; 70 feet wide. Steam turbines, single screw. Service speed 16.5 knots. 119 all-first-class passengers.]

SANTA ISABEL. The Grace Line built nine new combo ships just after the war. Six of them—*Santa Barbara, Santa Cecilia, Santa Isabel* **(opposite, top)**, *Santa Luisa, Santa Margarita,* and *Santa Maria*—were assigned to the forty-two-day round-trip voyage from New York via the Panama Canal to ports along the west coast of South America. The remaining, slightly different three (*Santa Clara, Santa Monica,* and *Santa Sofia*) ran eighteen-day sailings to the Caribbean and Venezuela. Among their amenities was a movie-screen mounted on the aft mast and used for open-air screenings. [Built by North Carolina Shipbuilding Corporation, Wilmington, North Carolina, 1946. 8,357 gross tons; 459 feet long; 63 feet wide. Steam turbines, single screw. Service speed 16 knots. 52 all-first-class passengers.]

EXCAMBION and **EXOCHORDA.** Four of the most successful U.S.-flag combination ships were American Export Lines' postwar "Four Aces," the *Excalibur, Excambion, Exeter,* and *Exochorda.* They had been built as Navy attack transports, the USS *Duchess,* USS *Queens,* USS *Shelby,* and USS *Dauphin,* respectively, and all were converted to passenger ships in 1948 and were said to offer some of the finest accommodations to put to sea in the late 1940s. They had splendid public rooms and an outdoor pool, and all cabins had private bath. They were the first fully air conditioned commercial passenger ships in the world. The "Four Aces" ran a very popular six-week round-trip service from New York Harbor (from Jersey City, later from Hoboken) to the Mediterranean (Cadiz, Barcelona, Marseilles, Naples, Alexandria, Beirut, Naples, Marseilles, Genoa, Leghorn, Barcelona, and home via Boston). On June 27, 1950, the *Excalibur* collided with the Danish-flag freighter *Colombia* within an hour after leaving her New Jersey pier *(below).* The collision occurred off Brooklyn, and the American Export ship, with serious port side damages, immediately took on water and was down by the bow. Along with a small flotilla of harbor tugs and U.S. Coast Guard craft, a New York Central Railroad tug and covered freight barge were able to take on some of the damaged ship's cargo. Refloated, the *Excalibur* was repaired and later resumed her posted schedule.

In the face of airline competition and American Export's decision to build new, faster, more efficient twelve-passenger freighters, the *Excambion* and *Exochorda* were withdrawn in 1958. After some time in the Hudson River reserve fleet, the *Excambion* became the cadet training ship *Texas Clipper* for Texas A&M University, and the *Exochorda* went to Stevens Institute of Technology for use as a permanently berthed student dormitory, the *Stevens*, at Hoboken, shown in this aerial view (*above*). She was removed in 1975 and scrapped four years later, but the *Texas Clipper* was still afloat in 1999, in layup at Beaumont, Texas.

The *Excalibur* (which survived a kitchen fire while at sea in 1963) and the *Exeter* were retired by American Export in 1964, then later sold to Taiwanese shipping tycoon C. Y. Tung for his Orient Overseas Line division. They sailed in further passenger-cargo service, from San Francisco to the Far East, before being broken up in 1974. [Built by Bethlehem Steel Company, Sparrows Point, Maryland, 1944. 9,644 gross tons; 473 feet long; 66 feet wide. Steam turbines, single screw. Service speed 17 knots. 125 all-first-class passengers.]

ALCOA CAVALIER. The Alcoa Steamship Company, an arm of the Aluminum Company of America, had a trio of combination ships in service out of New Orleans. The *Alcoa Cavalier* (*below*), *Alcoa Clipper*, and *Alcoa Corsair* were built upon standardized Victory Ship hulls, then were completed with a good use of aluminum in their superstructure. Thus, they were something of a showcase for their owners' main product. The ships sailed on three-week itineraries, from New Orleans to Kingston, Santo Domingo, San Juan, Puerto Cabello, La Guaira, Guanta, and Port of Spain. There they loaded their most important cargo, bauxite, the chief ingredient in aluminum. The ships returned to the U.S. directly, first to Mobile and then New Orleans. By the time these Alcoa ships were retired in 1960, the age of the American combination passenger-ship was closing. Such ships had become too expensive to operate compared to larger passenger liners and the new generation of more efficient cargo vessels. [Built by Oregon Shipbuilding Corporation, Portland, Oregon, 1947. 8,481 gross tons; 455 feet long; 62 feet wide. Steam turbines, single screw. Service speed 16.5 knots. 95 all-first-class passengers.]

CHAPTER 9

Serving the Military During and After World War II

After the outbreak of war in Europe in 1939, almost all passenger ship services were brought to a halt. American vessels continued to operate on the North Atlantic for some time, however, bringing anxious tourists and refugees to the U.S. Even small liners designed for coastal sailing were pressed into service, joining the likes of far larger ships such as the *Manhattan* and the *Washington* in making these important voyages. But it was not long before these American ships were called into military service, painted gray or in wartime camouflage, and refitted to carry many more passengers in much less comfort. The 1,046-passenger *America*, for example, had an official troopship capacity of 8,175. With the exception of dining rooms converted to mess halls, just about every available space on board was converted to multibunk accommodations. The officers shared staterooms, the G.I.s crowded into tiers of hammocks.

Many ships in the process of being built were redesigned for military service; indeed, some never saw a day of commercial service. Entire projects never came to fruition. Among the latter were new combination classes scheduled to be built for such lines as American Merchant and Moore McCormack. Pressed by the need to deliver hundreds of thousands of troops and mountains of supplies to overseas locations, the U.S. government also used many foreign and formerly foreign ships, For example, in 1942 Washington made an outright purchase of Sweden's *Kungsholm*, which became a troopship, appropriately renamed USS *John Ericsson*. Another source of tonnage was ships that had been seized or interned after the outbreak of hostilities. The Italian liners *Conte Biancamano* and *Conte Grande* were converted to the troopers USS *Hermitage* and USS *Monticello*, and the ex-German liner *Windhuk* became the USS *Lejeune*. Another German contribution to the Allied cause came late, in May 1945, when the third largest liner afloat, the *Europa*, was seized in the capture of the city of Bremerhaven. Another superliner, the French Line's *Normandie*, was seized at her New York pier shortly after the U.S. entered the war. Great expectations went up in flames in 1942, when this great ship was virtually destroyed by a fire that occurred as she was being refitted as a troopship. The greatest of them all, the British-owned *Queen Mary* and *Queen Elizabeth*, by themselves carried hundreds of thousands of troops from the United States into the battle zones.

The high pitch of American industrial productivity during the war years gave rise to the construction of several sets of specialized troopships. The biggest of these ships were of the General class—being named after U.S. Army general officers. Eleven of these P2-S2-R2 ships were built during this period, along with eight slightly smaller, differently configured vessels of the Admiral class, designated P2-SE2-R1. In addition, thirty of the engines-aft C4-S-A1 class were built, as well as fifteen of a slightly modified group of the same class. "These ships were all tremendously important to the war effort and to the quick end to that conflict," according to Frank O. Braynard. "The 'Generals' and the 'Admirals' were specially built on different coasts so as to be ready for immediate service either in the Atlantic or the Pacific. These twin-funnel ships were so much like actual liners that they were the basis for our postwar liners, ships such as the *President Cleveland* and the *Independence*. Actually, the government had hoped that more of the 'General' class in particular would be converted and used commercially after the war was over. In reality, because of their very high operational costs, particularly in fuel consumption, only three actually saw service with commercial companies."

Many of these troopships remained in military service long after World War II. Dozens of ships continued their transportation duties, carrying not only service personnel and their families but also refugees and displaced persons. In 1949 the Military Sea Transportation Service (MSTS) was created to administer what had become a worldwide network of shipping services. Gray-painted still, and with generally spartan accommodations designed to move the greatest number at the lowest cost in the fastest time, these ships did yeoman's service until the early 1970s. By then the preferred method of transportation was by air, administered by the Air Transport Command. By the spring of 1973 the fleet of troopships was down to one, the USS *Barrett*, Soon she was decommissioned as well. Only a handful of these aging troop transports are still in existence, most of them in "mothball fleets" awaiting their day with the scrappers.

GEORGE CLYMER. The great American shipbuilding program of the late 1930s that sparked the growth of the U.S. merchant marine came at an opportune time—just as World War II erupted in the late summer of 1939. As the United States itself became enmeshed in the conflict, the government needed more and more ships to transport troops and supplies overseas. In June 1941, for example, six months before America officially entered the conflict, the military began taking over commercial vessels. Brand-new ships were no exception. American President Lines' combo ship *President Adams*, for example, was requisitioned by the Navy, redesigned during construction, and then completed as a transport. When the U.S. entered the war after the Japanese attack on Pearl Harbor, on December 7, 1941, there were no less than seventeen passenger ships under construction. Four of the intended *Rio Hudson* class of passenger-cargo ships, building at Chester, Pennsylvania, for Moore-McCormack Lines, were finished as escort aircraft carriers. Many other ships intended for commercial passenger service were also quickly redesigned for various military purposes. Sadly, many of them were never restored.

The American South African Line, better known as the Farrell Lines, was building a trio of superb combination ships for its services between New York and African ports. They were the *African Comet, African Meteor,* and *African Planet,* each designed to carry 100 all-first-class passengers in splendid accommodations. The *African Comet,* launched in June, 1941, even had some historical significance: She was the first passenger ship with an all-welded hull. The *Comet* was completely fitted out and ready for commercial service when called to duty—her gala maiden voyage never took place. The other sisters did not get that far. The *African Planet,* for example, was renamed USS *George Clymer* by the U.S. Navy and was commissioned for transport service in June 1942. The *Clymer* is in the foreground of the photo *(above),* with other military ships at anchor. Laid up after the war and never restored for any further sailings, she was finally declared surplus and broken up at San Pedro, California, in the summer of 1968. The two other sisters faced a similar fate, but at the hands of Texas shipbreakers in 1973. [Built by Ingalls Shipbuilding Corporation, Pascagoula, Mississippi, 1942. 10,812 gross tons; 489 feet long; 69 feet wide. Steam turbines, single screw. Service speed 19 knots. 100 all-first-class passengers as intended.]

PVT. ELDEN H. JOHNSON. The Alcoa Steamship Company had three ships on the ways in the final months of 1941, *Alcoa Courier*, *Alcoa Corsair*, and *Alcoa Cruiser*. Intended for passenger service to the Caribbean, they were soon taken over and redesigned by the Navy for use as armed hospital transports. They were renamed USS *Tryon*, USS *Pinkney*, and USS *Rixey*, respectively, and went into service in the second half of 1942. After the war they were transferred to the U.S. Army and again renamed, this time as the USS *Sgt. Charles E. Mower*, USS *Pvt. Elden H. Johnson*, and USS *Pvt. William H. Thomas*. They were used by the MSTS, the Military Sea Transportation Service, to carry not only peacetime troops but dependent families as well. All were decommissioned by 1959 and spent the next decade or so in reserve. The *Johnson* and the *Thomas*, shown *(above)* nested alongside each other in the Hudson River, were ultimately sold to Taiwanese scrappers. They were demolished in 1971. [Built by Moore Dry Dock Company, Oakland, California, 1942. 7,486 gross tons; 450 feet long; 62 feet wide. Steam turbines, single screw. Service speed 20 knots. 95 all-first-class passengers as intended.]

DAVID C. SHANKS. The United States Lines had planned a quartet of passenger-cargo ships for their American Merchant Lines' division. They were to be *American Merchant*, *American Banker*, *American Shipper*, and *American Farmer*, but they never saw a day of commercial use. In 1941 they were taken over by the U.S. Army and completed as troop transports. The intended *American Farmer*, for example, was launched as the USS *Gulfport*, then completed as the USS *David C. Shanks*. She is shown *(below)* arriving at Bethlehem Steel's San Francisco yard for repairs in the late 1940s, wearing the funnel colors of the Army Transport Service. Her capacity, intended to be 165 civilians in all-first-class quarters, soared to 2,000 during the war, then was reduced to some 500 in postwar service. She too later sailed for MSTS, mostly on transpacific voyages. Laid up in 1959, she was idle for fourteen years before being broken up in Taiwan. [Built by Ingalls Shipbuilding Corporation, Pascagoula, Mississippi, 1942. 11,900 gross tons; 492 feet long; 70 feet wide. Steam turbines, single screw. Service speed 17 knots. 165 all-first-class passengers as intended.]

Serving the Military During and After World War II

BLANCHE F. SIGMAN. Even though Liberty ships had a low minimum speed (a scant eleven knots at best), the U.S. government decided to convert six of them into military transports and hospital ships. The *Blanche F. Sigman,* shown **(opposite, top)** arriving in New York in 1945, had been completed as the Liberty *Stanford White* and operated as a cargo ship for several months before being selected for conversion at the Todd shipyards in Hoboken. Initially, it was intended to rename her *Poppy.* Hospital ships were supposedly exempt from enemy attack. They even had illuminated red crosses along their sides and on their upper decks, and their crews were civilians. Facilities included wards, operating rooms, and hospital-type kitchens. The *Sigman's* operations were managed by the New York-based United States Lines. She made numerous transatlantic crossings, to the Mediterranean, Great Britain, and, in 1945–46, to and from a defeated Germany. Laid up in 1946, she spent some years in mothballs before being sent to the scrappers. [Built by California Shipbuilding Corporation, Los Angeles, California, 1943. 7,933 gross tons; 441 feet long; 57 feet wide. Steam triple-expansion engines, single screw. Service speed 11 knots. 595 patients.]

JOHN ERICSSON. The U.S. government not only operated some foreign-flag passenger ships as troop carriers during the war years, but also purchased others outright. The Swedish American Line's *Kungsholm* was bought just after the attack on Pearl Harbor and was renamed the *John Ericcson (opposite, bottom)* in honor of the nineteenth-century Swedish designer of the USS *Monitor.* Managed by the United States Lines, she made two Pacific voyages and twenty-seven to Europe and Africa as a troopship. She sailed from New York to the likes of Belfast, Greenock, Liverpool, and Marseilles, as well as to Freetown (Sierra Leone) and as far south as Capetown, South Africa. Damaged by a fire while berthed at New York's Pier 90 in March 1947, she was sold back to her original owners, who resold her to the newly formed Home Lines, a company in which the Swedes had a financial interest. She was

refitted for commercial passenger service as the liner *Italia.* Used in transatlantic and later cruise services, she endured until broken up in Spain in 1965. [Built by Blohm & Voss Shipbuilders, Hamburg, Germany, 1928. 20,223 gross tons; 609 feet long; 78 feet wide. Burmeister & Wain diesels, twin screw. Service speed 17.5 knots. 1,575 passengers in peacetime; 5,461 troops during the war.]

HERMITAGE. Among other foreign liners used by the U.S. during the war were the Italian Line near-sisterships *Conte Biancamano* and *Conte Grande.* Known for their fine service, cuisine, and exceptional decor, they were "floating palazzi." But then came the war. Laid up in the Panama Canal Zone in the spring of 1940, the *Biancamano* was seized by the Americans in March 1941. (She was among twenty-eight Italian ships taken by U.S. authorities in territorial waters.) Later renamed USS *Hermitage,* she was outfitted as a large troopship at the Philadelphia Navy Yard **(above),** where she is seen departing on August 17, 1942. Her capacity soared from 1,750 in peacetime to 6,107 in wartime. She sailed mostly in Pacific waters at first, but then moved to the Atlantic, crossing to the likes of Liverpool and Le Havre, Marseilles and Oran. In 1946 she was sent back to the Pacific, on voyages to occupied Japan. Decommissioned in the summer of 1947, she was later returned to her Italian owners and was thoroughly restored, although with far more contemporary quarters. As the *Conte Biancamano* she sailed in and out of the Mediterranean, mostly to ports along the east coast of South America, but also occasionally on a northern course to Halifax and New York. The *Conte Grande* had been seized by Brazilian authorities early in the war and was sold, in April 1942, to the U.S. government. She became the USS *Monticello,* another highly valuable trooper. She too was later returned to the Italians and reconditioned under her original name. [*Conte Biancamano:* Built by William Beardmore & Company Limited, Glasgow, Scotland, 1925. 24,416 gross tons; 653 feet long; 78 feet wide. Steam turbines, twin screw. Service speed 20 knots. 1,750 passengers in peacetime; 6,107 in wartime.]

THE "QUEENS" IN WAR.

THE "QUEENS" IN WAR. The three largest ocean liners afloat came under some American control during the war. The magnificent French Line flagship *Normandie*, often said to be the most luxurious passenger ship ever built, was laid up at New York in August 1939 and then seized by the U.S. in December 1941. (The Germans had set up their puppet government in Vichy, France, in 1940.) The *Normandie* was renamed USS *Lafayette* and was being transformed into a 15,000-capacity troopship at her French Line berth on the Hudson River at West 48th Street, when she caught fire, on February 9, 1942. Later she capsized and had to be partially scrapped so as to be righted. By then, however, in the fall of 1943, her value had so diminished that she was laid up. Finally, in 1946, her hull was sold to local New York scrappers.

Great Britain's *Queen Mary* and *Queen Elizabeth*, equal in size and speed to their French rival, were invaluable troopers throughout the war. In their gray paint, stripped of most finery and reconfigured for maximum military use, they roamed the globe at first, but beginning in 1942 they stayed mostly on the North Atlantic. Between December 1942 and April 1943, both ships worked in tandem between New York and Greenock in Scotland, carried a total of 105,000 troops and steamed some 339,000 miles. For every eastbound voyage a whole division of infantry could be taken into the battle zone. In July 1943 the *Queen Mary* left New York's Pier 90 with 16,683 souls on board, a record that holds to this day. On another occasion, with a combined 15,000 troops and crew aboard, there was only one woman aboard. She was given special protection during the five-day run up to the Clyde. In this view (*above*) the aftdecks of the *Queen Mary* are seen during a post war sailing from Europe to New York.

Both the *Queen Mary* and the *Queen Elizabeth* were loaned to the U.S. government during the war, but they remained British ships, owned by the Cunard-White Star Line. The ships were considered part of what was called a "reverse lend lease." But to the hundreds of thousands of Yanks who crossed in the two mighty liners, the *Mary* and the *Elizabeth* could only be American ships. "After all, who else could build such giant vessels?" noted one officer. A shopping list for one of the *Queen's* five-day crossings during the war was staggering by any standard: 124,000 lb. potatoes, 29,000 lb. fresh fruit, 18,000 lb. jam, 155,000 lb. meat and poultry, 76,000 lb. flour and cereal, and 31,000 lb. sugar, tea, and coffee. There were nineteen canteens aboard those big Cunarders, selling soft drinks, cigarettes, and candies, but absolutely no chewing gum. The sticky wads were a nuisance to the Cunard crews who spent hours scraping them from decks, piping, overheads, and handrails.

After returning servicemen from Europe to America in 1945–46, the Queens were returned to Cunard and restored for luxury, three-class passenger service. The *Mary* sailed until 1967, when she was sold and converted to a hotel-museum at Long Beach, California; the *Elizabeth*, retired a year later, was to have become a Chinese-owned cruise-ship-floating-university combination, but, sadly, she burned at Hong Kong in January 1972 and was scrapped. [*Queen Mary*: Built by John Brown & Company Limited, Clydebank, Scotland, 1930–36. 81,235 gross tons; 1,018 feet long; 118 feet wide; 39-foot draft. Steam turbines, quadruple screw. Service speed 28.5 knots (often increased during the War). 2,139 peacetime passengers as built; 15,000-plus troops during the war.]

RECORD NUMBERS. A Pennsylvanian, Paul S. Shimer, Jr., became the "millionth Yank" to embark from a port in southern England *(above)*. Such a notation was recorded, in a slight hint of less restrictive publicity and security, on November 25, 1944.

TAKASAGO MARU. The Allies, particularly the Americans, were involved with the disposition and immediate operation of tonnage of the defeated Axis nations. The Japanese, for example, had only one notable passenger ship, the 11,000-ton *Hikawa Maru*, still afloat. U.S. occupation authorities allowed her only to sail local waters, between the Japanese islands, and it was not until the early 1950s that she was permitted to resume deep-sea service between Kobe, Yokohama, Honolulu, Vancouver, and Seattle. The Germans resumed their transatlantic service to New York with the first sailing in 1955 of the *Berlin*, the former Swedish *Gripsholm*.

Another Japanese liner that came under Allied control after the war was the hospital ship *Takasago Maru*. She had been built in 1936 for commercial service, sailing between Kobe, Moji, and Keelung, but then was transferred, in 1940, to the Imperial Japanese Navy for use in hospital services. After the war, as seen in this aerial view dated August 30, 1945 *(below)*, she was pressed into repatriation service, returning Japanese soldiers and civilians detained in Siberia, and those living in Manchuria, China, and the Southeast Asian territories. There were also plans to restore her as a passenger ship, carrying mostly Japanese immigrants, to the east coast of South America, but this never came to pass. She was a coal-burner, and the cost of converting her to oil was too great in a ravaged Japan of the late 1940s. Instead, she was laid up and subsequently sold to scrappers at Osaka in 1956. [Built by Mitsubishi Shipbuilding & Engineering Company, Nagasaki, Japan, 1936. 9,315 gross tons; 460 feet long; 62 feet wide. Steam turbines, twin screw. Service speed 15 knots. 856 prewar passengers (45 first class, 156 second class, 700 third class).]

GENERAL J. C. BRECKINRIDGE. Beginning in 1942–43, America embarked on a specific program of building troopships of varied sizes. Some were intended to continue in military service once the war was over, but others were designed for eventual conversion to commercial services. The largest of these ships was the P2-S2-R2 class, a point reinforced by a pair of deliberately powerful-looking stacks atop a rather minimal superstructure. The eleven ships of this class, which were intended for U.S. Navy operation, were built on the East Coast and so were planned more specifically for transatlantic duties. Each was named after an American general. Designed without portholes and so fully air conditioned (the first large passenger-carrying vessels of any type to have this distinction), they carried up to 6,000 passengers in wartime, a number reduced to approximately 4,000 and later 2,000 in the subsequent postwar years.

July 13, 1945: the *General J. C. Breckinridge (above)* is about to pass under the 130-foot-high railway lift bridge across Newark Bay. She has just been completed by United States Steel's Federal Shipyard at Kearny, New Jersey, and is heading for her first sailing, as the last of this class. Three additional ships of this class had been ordered, but these orders were canceled owing to the end of the war in Europe. In the ensuing months the *Breckinridge* crossed the Atlantic numerous times, sailing to Marseilles or Le Havre. This tour of duty was followed by voyages in the Pacific, to the likes of Manila, Guam, Saipan, and Shanghai. In 1949 she was among the many transports assigned to MSTS, the Military Sea Transportation Service, for worldwide services carrying American troops as well as dependents.

There had been hope from the start that at least some of these P2-S2-R2 ships would be used in postwar commercial service, to help revive the American passenger ship industry. They were thought to be ideal for the likes of the United States Lines on the often gruelling North Atlantic run to Southampton, Le Havre, and Bremerhaven. They were also thought to be well suited as passenger ships for the Farrell Lines to South and East Africa, for the Grace Line to the Caribbean and South America, and for the Moore-McCormack Lines to the east coast of South America as well as for their American Scantic Line subsidiary's service to Baltic ports and Norway. In fact, there would be less than enthusiastic interest in these vessels by U.S. shipowners after the war, in the late 1940s. One of this class, the *General W. P. Richardson* was experimentally converted to a commercial liner in 1948–49. She was later run as the *La Guardia* for American Export Lines on their transatlantic service between New York and the Mediterranean, but with very limited success. The *General W. H. Gordon* was to follow as a conversion, but received only minimal upgrading. The *General M. C. Meigs* was to have been the third conversion, but she remained completely untouched. [Built by Federal Shipbuilding & Dry Dock Company, Kearny, New Jersey, 1945. 17,800 gross tons; 622 feet long; 75 feet wide. Steam turbines, twin screw. Service speed 19 knots. Approximately 6,000 troops in wartime; reduced to about 4,000 in peacetime.]

GENERAL WILLIAM WEIGEL. Shown during Navy Day maneuvers in New York's Lower Bay, just across from the Statue of Liberty, the *General William Weigel* (*above*) actually spent most of her postwar years under MSTS operation in the Pacific. She sailed from San Francisco and sometimes Seattle to the likes of Yokohama and Kobe, Okinawa, Manila, Subic Bay, Pusan, Inchon, Honolulu, and Guam. Of course, ships such as this were particularly useful in the early 1950s during the Korean War. Laid up in the 1960s, as the government began to wind down troopship operations, ships like the *Weigel* spent time in reserve fleets before being auctioned off to scrappers. By 1998 the last surviving member of this P2-S2-R2 class, the *General John Pope*, was still moored in the Federal Reserve Fleet at Suisun Bay, California. However, she has been placed on the U.S. Maritime Commission's "disposal list" and most likely will be sold to shipbreakers in the not-too-distant future. [Built by Federal Shipbuilding & Dry Dock Company, Kearny, New Jersey, 1944. 17,800 gross tons; 622 feet long; 75 feet wide. Steam turbine, twin screw. Service speed 19 knots. Approximately 6,000 troops during wartime; reduced to approximately 4,000 and later 2,000 in peacetime.]

GENERAL HUGH J. GAFFEY. Just after the United States entered the War, planning was begun for a series of troopships just slightly smaller than the aforementioned P2-S2-R2 class. Ships of the new P2-SE2-R1 type were intended primarily for Pacific service. Ten ships of this class were ordered, but the last two were canceled and then sold as unfinished hulls to American President, who had them redesigned as the liners *President Cleveland* and *President Wilson*. The earlier eight sisterships of this group were completed with admiral names, first for the Army, then for the Navy, but then, in 1946–47, back to the Army. The admiral names were soon changed to those of generals. The *General Hugh J. Gaffey*, for example, had been completed in September 1944 as the *Admiral W. L. Capps*. She is seen (*below*) in U.S. Army Transport Service colors, August 16, 1948, at the Newport News Shipyard in Virginia. Like all of her troop-carrying sisterships, she was transferred to MSTS operation by 1950. [Built by Bethlehem-Alameda Shipyard Inc., Alameda, California, 1944. Approximately 16,000 gross tons; 609 feet long; 75 feet wide. Steam turboelectric, twin screw. Service speed 19 knots. Approximately 5,000 troops in wartime; reduced to about 2,000 in later peacetime service.]

GENERAL WILLIAM O. DARBY. After duties in the Second World War and then repatriation sailings after 1945, these "general" class troopships, the largest and most powerful in the U.S. government's fleet, were refitted and made more comfortable. On the Atlantic they generally sailed from the Brooklyn Army Terminal to either Southampton or Bremerhaven or, on occasion, to Rota in Spain. By the 1960s some of the MSTS troopers, such as the *General William O. Darby*, were refitted to make government travel "more pleasant and appetizing." This view *(left),* shows the ship's refurbished dining room. [Built by Bethlehem-Alameda Shipyard Inc., Alameda, California, 1945. Approximately 16,000 gross tons; 609 feet long, 75 feet wide. Steam turboelectric, twin screw. Service speed 19 knots. Approximately 5,000 troops in wartime, reduced to about 2,000 in later peacetime service.]

FINAL DAYS. At its peak, in the early 1950s, MSTS was operating fifty-eight troop-carrying ships. But by the 1960s this had been greatly reduced, especially as military personnel and their families were using aircraft more and more. Many ships were being decommissioned. In this aerial view *(above),* taken off Caven Point, Jersey City, in New York's Lower Bay, four troopers have finished their last MSTS sailings and are about to be sent to the reserve fleet in the James River. At the far left is the *General Simon B. Buckner* with the *General Alexander M. Patch* just behind, then the *General William O. Darby* with the *General Maurice Rose* behind her. When I visited the *Patch* and the *Rose,* still laid up in Virginia on a winter's day in 1980, their passenger quarters were virtually untouched: furniture in place, notices posted on bulletin boards, an old projector in the auditorium. Dishes were stacked on a serving counter, cutlery filled some drawers, and children's high chairs were stored against a bulkhead. The *Darby* eventually became a stripped-down barracks ship for the Navy, while the others eventually went on the "disposal list." In the summer of 1997, for example, both the *Buckner* and the *Darby* were to be towed to Brownsville, Texas, for scrapping.

GENERAL W. M. BLACK. Thirty troopships of the C4-S-A1 class were commissioned between October 1943 and September 1945, all built by industrialist Henry J. Kaiser's special wartime shipbuilding plant at Richmond, California. Very functional ships in almost every way, this class used an engines-aft design that was capped by a very small, tin-can-like stack. Wartime capacity went up to 3,000, and there was a crew of 250. After the war, while in MSTS service, the total capacity was often reduced by more than half. Some were laid up soon after the war, while others were used during the 1950s and into the '60s. Some of these ships were used on rather special voyages: carrying immigrants and refugees, even displaced persons. In this view *(above)*, dated October 31, 1948, the *General W. M. Black* is arriving in late afternoon off Lower Manhattan, bound for Pier 84. Bedecked in flags for the occasion, she is landing the first load of displaced persons, over 800 in all, to reach New York since the end of the war. At this time refugees were not popular with the American public. Thus, many subsequent landings were made quietly, at remote New York harbor berths such as Brooklyn's Red Hook, the Brooklyn Army Terminal, or Staten Island's Stapleton piers.

The *General Black* was laid up in 1956 in the Suisun Bay reserve fleet. A decade later she was put up for sale and acquired by the U.S.-flag Central Gulf Steamship Company, who had her rebuilt as a heavy-lift freighter, the *Green Forest*. In place of the former troop quarters there were now cargo holds and three fifty-ton heavy-lift derricks. She ended her days in January 1980, when she was handed over to scrappers at Kaohsiung, Taiwan. [Built by the Kaiser Company Incorporated, Richmond, California, 1944. 10,600 gross tons; 523 feet long; 72 feet wide. Steam turbines, twin screw. Service speed 17 knots. Up to 3,000 troops during wartime.]

CONVERSION. Almost unrecognizable, the former C4-type troopship *General D. E. Aultman* was laid up in 1958. She was lengthened by over 150 feet a decade later in a conversion to the container-cargo ship *Portland* *(left)*. Sea-Land Service, her new owner, was an American shipping firm that was the pioneer of containerized cargo transport in the mid-1950s. These converted ships later gave way to even larger, custom-built container ships.

PRESIDENT ADAMS/GEIGER. The rebuilding program sponsored by the federal government to revive the American passenger ship industry after the Second World War included a trio of combination passenger-cargo ships. These last-named vessels, intended for American President Lines, were the very last full-time troopships to sail under the U.S. flag. The *President Jackson*, the *President Adams* (*top*) being launched at Camden, New Jersey, on October 9, 1950, and the *President Hayes* were each built to carry 204 passengers in luxurious quarters on continuous three-month voyages around the world. But following the outbreak of war in Korea, the three incomplete ships were requisitioned by the government and converted to troopships, the *Barrett*, *Geiger*, and *Upshur*, respectively. [Built by the New York Shipbuilding Corporation, Camden, New Jersey, 1951. 13,300 gross tons; 553 feet long; 73 feet wide. Steam turbines, single screw. Service speed 20 knots. 1,896 passengers (396 dependent passengers, 1,500 troops).]

EMPIRE STATE. The *Barrett*, *Geiger*, and *Upshur* sailed in MSTS service even after the end of the conflict in Korea. The *Barrett* tended to work in the Pacific, whereas the other two were familiar sights in New York, sailing to northern Europe, to Spain, and on occasion to Puerto Rico. The *Geiger* was the first to be retired, laid up in April 1971. The *Barrett* and *Upshur* followed two years later. In fact, it was the *Barrett* that landed the last U.S. servicemen to go by sea when she arrived at Los Angeles in March 1973. After their time as troopers, the three ships had diverse careers. The *Barrett* became the cadet training ship *Empire State* (*bottom*) for the New York State Maritime College. She was retired in 1989, and placed in the reserve fleet in the James River, Virginia. More recently, she served as a training site for U.S. Navy assault teams, but as of 1998, she was on the "disposal list," for scrapping.

The *Upshur* was transferred to the Maine Maritime Academy and became the training ship *State of Maine*. In 1995 she sailed to Mobile, Alabama, where the U.S. Coast Guard employed her for firefighter training. Controlled fires are still staged within her superstructure and cargo holds. The *Geiger* was laid up until 1980, when she too became a training ship, the *Bay State*, for the Massachusetts Maritime Academy. But on December 22, 1981, she was seriously damaged by an engine room fire and had to be sold to scrappers.

CHAPTER 10

Modern American Luxury at Sea

In many ways American passenger ships reached their peak after the Second World War, particularly in the 1950s. Sea travel was still popular, postwar prosperity was rolling along in spite of periodic recessions, and the prejet piston-driven airlines remained only a distant threat. "America in the 1950s was not only a military superpower, but an industrial power as well," noted Jack Weatherford. "Ships like the record-breaking *United States* were symbols of this overall superiority. She represented not only American technology but also the American economy and the American way of life. Of course, the politicians who underwrote the building of such ships feared another war. The Cold War was very real. Ocean liners could be troopships. But it was the last hurrah for these ships. The North Atlantic run and others soon fell into decline. Air transport was the future. During the Kennedy era there were new projects such as landing a man on the moon. There was no focus on water or on ships."

Toward the end of the Second World War the Roosevelt Administration planned for no less than eleven large new ocean liners. Again, their alternative use as troopships in time of war was surely an important factor. But by 1946 the Truman Administration had already scaled back these plans to include only six ships: one superliner for the North Atlantic (the *United States*), two medium-sized liners for mid-Atlantic sailings to the Mediterranean (the *Independence* and the *Constitution*), and three combination passenger-cargo vessels for around-the-world service (American President Lines' *President Jackson*, *President Adams*, and *President Hayes*).

Added to the many new American combination freight and passenger ships were other new liners such as the sisterships *President Cleveland* and *President Wilson* (1947-48). They were followed by the *Independence* and *Constitution* (both 1951) and the greatest of them all, the magnificent *United States* (1952). "These ships brought America to the 'A-class' of ocean liners after the war. They were top echelon," said Frank O. Braynard. "The *United States* was absolutely overwhelming. She was the greatest newly built American passenger ship in one hundred years, since the paddlewheeler *Baltic* of 1852, which belonged to the old Collins Line. She, too, was the fastest ship of her time. Both ships were great symbols of American might and power and victory. The *United States* was hailed even by the rival British."

But then too many strikes, increasing labor and fuel costs, and finally too few passengers killed off almost all U.S.-flag passenger ships in the 1960s and early '70s. So many milestones were passed, so many changes were made. The *United States* closed out over a century of American service on the North Atlantic run with a final voyage in 1969. The sisterships *Mariposa* and *Monterey* ended transpacific sailings in 1977-78. All that remained was the sailings of the aging *Independence* in cruise service around the Hawaiian islands. Through the 1980s and early '90s it was believed by most observers that the golden era of American oceangoing passenger service was just about over. But then the cruise industry began a boom that continued to accelerate into the 21st century. Based in such ports as Miami and Port Everglades, Florida, cruise lines began ordering new ships to accommodate an ever-increasing passenger load. The new fleet was highlighted by twin 71,000-tonners, the largest U.S.-built liners ever, for Hawaiian sailings. They were scheduled to be on the high seas sometime in 2003.

PRESIDENT CLEVELAND. Two troop transports, the intended *Admiral D. W. Taylor* and *Admiral F. B. Upham*, both of the P2-SE2-R1 class, were in fact too late for the war, and their incomplete hulls were offered for sale. Designed from the start for Pacific service, they seemed ideal for the American President Lines, anxious to resume service from California to the Far East via Hawaii. New designs were created, and the ships emerged in 1947–48 as the *President Cleveland* (**right**) and *President Wilson*, respectively. They were the first large American liners to come into service following the Second World War. When they first visited Asian ports, especially in devastated Japan, they were seen as "symbols of peace, goodwill and high American technology." The prewar rivals to American President Lines in the transpacific luxury trade were all but gone. Canadian Pacific decided not to resume its services from Vancouver, while Japan's Nippon Yusen Kaisha, the NYK Line, was down to one small passenger ship, the 11,000-ton *Hikawa Maru*. The only other passenger-carrying ships on the long-haul Pacific run were American military transports, one of which, the *General W. H. Gordon*, was teamed with the *Cleveland* and *Wilson*, but only with slightly upgraded, all-tourist-class, austerity berths. [Built by Bethlehem-Alameda Shipyard, Alameda, California, 1947. 18,962 gross tons; 609 feet long; 75 feet wide. Steam turboelectric, twin screw. Service speed 20 knots. 778 passengers (324 first class, 454 economy class).]

Luxury went back to sea in those immediate postwar years, as evidenced by the first-class main lounge aboard the *President Wilson* (**below, left**). The decor was often said to be 1940s moderne. It included sleek furniture, light colors, good use of mirrors, and indirect lighting. The overall tone was warm, bright, and inviting.

The Marine Verandah aboard the *President Cleveland* (**below, right**) had the decorative style of a swanky nightclub gone to sea. Note the piano and bandstand off to the right and the circular dance floor in the center. The large mirror on the far side makes the room appear larger. The floor is highly polished linoleum, while the ceiling has a unique addition for the late 1940s: a large air conditioning duct.

This first-class double room (*top*) on the upper deck of the *President Wilson* was spacious and included a full bathroom, closets, as well as a specially mounted Emerson radio. The Venetian blinds that cover the twin portholes give the room a hotel-like effect. These quarters were priced at $200 per person for the five-day passage between California and Hawaii in 1953 and at $600 per person for the two-week run to Japan.

The *President Cleveland* and the *President Wilson* were highly successful ships in the 1950s, even being featured in the television series *Oh Susanna*, which ran from 1956 until 1960. The two ships were routed from San Francisco and Los Angeles to Honolulu, then on to Yokohama, Kobe, Hong Kong, and Manila. A third liner was employed as well, initially the all-first-class *President Hoover* (the former *Panama* of 1939) and then the rebuilt, luxurious *President Roosevelt*, a former wartime troopship. The *Cleveland* (*bottom*) and the *Wilson* in particular were popular with tourists, government and military personnel, and migrants coming east to the United States. But by the 1960s the trade was falling away, mostly because of increasing airline competition. By the late 1960s American President liners turned more and more to all-first-class cruising with increasingly diverse itineraries. There were three-day cruises down to Ensenada in Baja California, seven days to the Mexican Riviera, two weeks to Alaska, and then deluxe eight- and ten-week cruises to Europe via the Panama Canal. But in 1972–73, their government operating subsidies ceased. American President had little choice but to pull out of their money-losing passenger ship business. The two presidents were sold to Hong Kong-based tycoon C. Y. Tung, who wanted to expand into the Pacific passenger and international cruise trades. The *President Cleveland*, which became the *Oriental Empress* for a Panamanian-flag Tung subsidiary, saw very little service. Fuel oil price increases (from $35 to $95 per ton in 1973) put operational profits out of reach. Within a year the former *Cleveland* was sold to Taiwanese scrap merchants. The *Wilson*, which made American President's last passenger ship sailing in April 1973, became the *Oriental President*. She was laid up in 1975, then sold to scrappers a decade later.

Three yards had bid for the prized contract to build these ships: Newport News, in Virginia; New York Shipbuilding, in New Jersey; and Bethlehem Steel, in Massachusetts. In the end, Beth Steel got the orders. The first keel plates for the *Independence* were laid on March 29, 1949, and work on the *Constitution* started that summer. The ships were to be launched approximately four months apart. Twelve thousand tons of steel went into each of the American Export sisters—roughly the equivalent of the metal in 8,000 1950 Fords. The ships were equipped with separate auxiliary engine rooms for safety, two types of radar, and fourteen watertight transverse bulkheads. When the *Constitution* was launched on July 12, 1949, nearly 26,000 lbs. of hard grease and 20,000 lbs. of slip grease were used on the ways at Bethlehem's Quincy plant (*opposite*). A bottle of California wine was used for the actual christening, as part of the "all-American" character of these liners and American Export's fervid promotion of them. [Built by the Bethlehem Steel Company, Quincy, Massachusetts, 1951. 30,293 gross tons; 683 feet long; 89 feet wide. Steam turbines, twin screw. Service speed 23 knots. 1,000 passengers (295 first class, 375 cabin class, 330 tourist class).]

Industrial might: fitting one of the two huge, three-bladed propellers (*top*) to the *Independence* in the spring of 1949.

The overall designs for the *Independence* and the *Constitution* were based on the 1944-built P2 type transports shown in Chapter 9. Of course, there were considerable refinements. The sleek superstructure of the new liners was dominated by twin, domed funnels (for which American Export created new funnel colors) and a single, raked mast above the wheelhouse section. There were four cargo holds, two forward and two aft, that were worked by sets of kingposts and booms. On December 7, 1950, the *Independence* became the "speed queen of the American Merchant Marine." That afternoon, during her trials off the Maine coast, she reached a top speed of 26.1 knots, a knot faster than the *America's* speed record set back in 1940. When the *Constitution* set off on her trials in May 1951, it was rumored at first that she would exceed the record set by the *Independence*. But that never came about. Shown (*bottom*) leaving Quincy on May 24th, the *Constitution's* trials, staged off the Massachusetts coast, were quite successful, but not record-setting. In sixteen months, however, the *Independence's* record would be broken by the startlingly high speeds of the far larger *United States*.

CONSTITUTION. The rebuilding program for the American passenger fleet after World War II included the nation's largest and finest liners destined for mid-Atlantic service to the Mediterranean rather than the busier, more traditional route to northern Europe. These ships were fast and luxurious, splendid examples of America's ingenuity in the late 1940s. Among other features the liners *Independence* and *Constitution* were the world's first fully air-conditioned luxury liners. They were part of the New York–based American Export Lines, and the contracts for their construction, worth close to $1 billion in today's currency, were signed in June 1948.

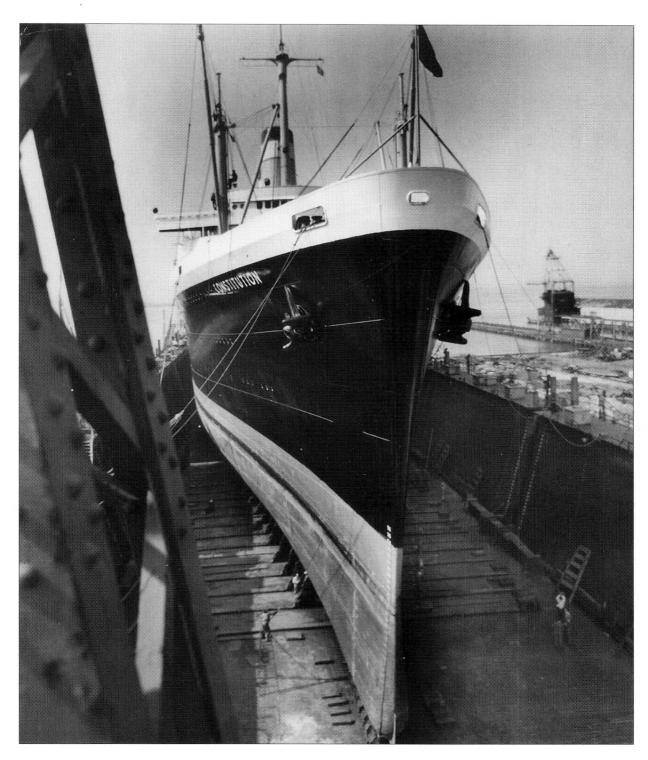

The *Independence* arrived at New York's Pier 84 at the foot of West 44th Street—current site of the *Intrepid* aircraft carrier museum—to a rousing welcome (*opposite, top*). Special guests had made the two-night voyage down from Boston to New York. "Big, powerful and luxurious—indeed, the perfect showcase for American technology and shipbuilding," was the judgment of critics.

The original three-bladed propellers aboard both the *Independence* (*opposite, bottom*) and the *Constitution* were, however, less than highly efficient and were soon replaced. Both liners took turns in the large dry dock at Bethlehem Steel's repair yard at 56th Street, Brooklyn, in the fall of 1951 and were given new five-

bladed props. They also had mid-winter stays at American Export's cargo terminal at Pier B in Hoboken for light maintenance, cleaning, and Coast Guard inspections.

Each winter both the *Independence* and *Constitution* had their annual overhauls in New York harbor. Whereas the likes of the *America* and the *United States* went to Newport News in Virginia each year, these American Export sisters sensibly used Bethlehem Steel facilities, first at their 56th Street plant in Brooklyn, where the *Constitution* is shown (*above*), September 21, 1951, and then, beginning in the mid-1960s, at Bethlehem's Hoboken, New Jersey, shipyard.

Industrial designer Henry Dreyfuss was entrusted with the interior design of the new American Export sisters. He had been hired with impressive credentials, having done the likes of the New York Central Railroad's luxurious *Twentieth Century Limited*, the Bell System's rotary telephone, Hoover vacuum cleaners, and Honeywell circular thermostats. His assignment was all-inclusive: fabrics, chinaware, cutlery, floor coverings, draperies, and lighting fixtures down to drawer pulls, stationery, and even matchbook covers. The atmosphere of "a fine American home" prevailed throughout the ship. Bright colors, which added to the overall sense of spaciousness, were used throughout, particularly in public areas such as the Independence Lounge aboard *(top)*.

Overall, the accommodations aboard the *Independence* were among the most modern afloat and included a large theater, a sunken-floor dining room, gymnasium, gift shops, elevators, and internal as well as ship-to-shore telephones. There were eight large suites, two of which had private verandas. The other cabins, which had private bathrooms, often included foldaway extra berths for third and even fourth passengers. Many cabins were convertible to daytime sitting rooms. There were two large pools aboard each ship. The first pool's lido area, as shown in this publicity photo *(middle)* of the *Independence*, was in the "Hollywood" style. The pool itself had rounded corners and could be illuminated for nighttime use. This area, which altogether covered some 9,000 square feet, included two broad wings one deck above for spectator viewing. Forward of the pool was the Sun Club Cafe, which included a Coca-Cola bar.

The enclosed promenade decks aboard the *Independence* **(bottom)** and the *Constitution* were popular for reading, strolls, and peaceful naps. These areas were also refuges from the often inclement Atlantic weather. The deck chairs were made of aluminum rather than the traditional teakwood. The tall windows along the sides could be opened to the soft sea breezes.

The *Independence* and the *Constitution* were immensely success-ful right from the start. American Export Lines generally kept to a three-week round-trip schedule with its two big liners, sailing them from New York to Algeciras, Spain, then on to Naples, Genoa, and Cannes, then back to New York. They sometimes passed each other in New York Harbor, as in this photo *(above)* taken on April 14, 1954, with the *Independence* on the right. Many passengers, even some Italian immigrants, liked the ships for their "American character." In the 1950s they often ran at over 90 percent of capac-ity. American Export's most serious competition came, of course, from the revived Italian Line, which added the stunning sisters *Andrea Doria* and *Cristoforo Colombo* in 1953–54, the larger *Leonardo da Vinci* in 1960, and finally the twin superliners *Michelangelo* and *Raffaello* in 1965.

The company had hoped for some time to have a third, large liner, perhaps even bigger than these ships, but U.S. government financial assistance was not forthcoming. Instead, by 1960, the converted freighter *Atlantic*, a smaller ship at 14,000 tons, was added for extended services to Greece and Israel. Fares in the early 1950s on the *Independence* and the *Constitution* started at $330 in first class, $260 in cabin class, and $205 in tourist. Among the more celebrated passengers were the kings of Morocco and Saudi Arabia, Mae West, Katharine Hepburn, Irving Berlin, and former President Harry Truman. Grace Kelly and her large bridal party of family and friends traveled aboard the *Constitution* to Monte Carlo in a specially arranged, highly publicized eastbound voyage in April 1956. The same ship was also the setting for several episodes of the *I Love Lucy* television series in 1955–56 and then in the original film of *An Affair to Remember* in 1956. The two sis-ters also made news when they docked without the assistance of tugs during strikes or when they themselves were idled by the fre-quent work stoppages by their all-American crews. In March 1959 the *Constitution* rammed and cut in two a Norwegian tanker, the *Jalanta*, outside New York Harbor. It was front-page news when it occurred and later, when an official board of inquiry found that the American Export Liner was at fault for going too fast.

Both the *Independence* and *Constitution*, seen (*above*) in the winter of 1966 along New York's "Luxury Liner Row" together with the *United States* and North German Lloyd's *Europa* (to the far right), were repainted with all-white hulls early in 1960. This gave the ships a tropical look, suggesting a more leisurely lifestyle at sea. By the 1960s they began to lose more Atlantic passengers to the airlines and, to some extent, to the newer Italian Line luxury ships. The American twins also began to lose more and more money. In an attempt to bring in more revenue, they were sent on one-class cruises, usually to Bermuda or farther south, to San Juan and St. Thomas. They were also booked by the likes of the Ford Motor Company for incentive cruises.

In April 1968, with deficits mounting, the *Independence* (*opposite, top*) came out of a Baltimore shipyard sporting a new $1 million "new look." In an effort to attract the younger "hip" market, the interiors were redecorated with bright colors, stripes, and bold carpets, while the exterior was given a "mod look" of sun rays that surrounded what were described as the eyes of 1930s film star Jean Harlow. The Italians called them "the evil eyes." Week-long cruises to the Caribbean were offered from $98 (or $14 per day), excluding food. But most passengers found themselves spending more than they would on an equivalent cruise. The *Independence*'s days as a psychedelic cruise ship were numbered. Moreover, in September 1968 the *Constitution* was laid up at Jacksonville, Florida; her sister followed in December, but to moorings at

Baltimore. America's second-largest liners were then put up for sale. Italian and Greek shipowners were among those who seemed interested, but not until 1974 were the ships sold to C. Y. Tung of Hong Kong. In 1970 the Chinese shipping magnate had bought the world's largest liner, Cunard's *Queen Elizabeth*, and had just about completed her conversion into the floating university cruise ship *Seawise University*, when she burned and capsized in Hong Kong harbor in January 1972.

The *Independence* and *Constitution* were placed under the Liberian flag for a Tung subsidiary, but they saw little service during the oil-expensive 1970s. In June 1980 the renamed *Oceanic Independence* (*opposite, bottom*) returned to U.S.-flag service for a new Tung division, American Hawaii Cruises, on seven-day inter-Hawaiian island cruises out of Honolulu. The *Oceanic Constitution* followed in 1982. Their names were soon shortened to the original *Independence* and *Constitution*, and they seemed to gain renewed popularity. The *Independence* was sent to the Newport News shipyard in Virginia in 1994 for an extensive and expensive life-extending refit. The *Constitution* was to follow, but the refit was delayed because of increased costs and a greater scope of work needed. Soon laid up at a Portland, Oregon, shipyard, the *Constitution* was eventually "cannibalized" for spare parts for her still-active sister before being sold to Far Eastern interests for scrap in October 1997. Weeks later, on November 17th, while under tow, she sank in the Pacific, northwest of Hawaii.

Gibbs was fascinated by funnels, especially big funnels. To him they conveyed an immediate impression of size, might, and great power. For the *United States*, he planned a pair of the largest funnels yet to put to sea. They would be pear-shaped and have smoke-deflecting fins at the top. Best of all, to Gibbs, they would be painted in his favorite colors: red, white, and blue. Even the steam whistles were important to him; they had to be the most powerful afloat. As seen in this photo (**opposite, top**) the top portion of the forward funnel is soon to be lifted by cranes and placed atop the base of the stack. The year is 1951.

UNITED STATES. William Francis Gibbs (**right**), perhaps the best known American naval architect of the 20th century, was trained as a lawyer. But he soon put aside the law and together with his brother Frederic opened the Gibbs Brothers Company in 1916. One of their first contracts was to convert the German liner *Vaterland* into the *Leviathan*. Gibbs later designed freighters, warships, ferries, and even fireboats, but he attracted the most attention with the *Malolo* of 1927, noteworthy for her advanced safety standards—another of his fascinations. In 1932–33 he produced a superb quartet of two-funnel liners for the Grace Line, the *Santa Rosa* class. In many ways, even at under 10,000 tons they were preludes to the overall designs of the Gibbs superliner. When he designed the *America* in the late 1930s, it was perhaps a "dry run" for this record-breaking megaship. Then war intervened. He and his firm, by then renamed Gibbs & Cox, turned their attention to the war effort and designed two-thirds of all merchant ships and three-quarters of all warships built from 1940 to 1945. But Gibbs still used off hours to work on sketches for the fastest liner of all. He began serious work in 1943, five years before such a ship's construction was even made public. The United States Lines authorized planning for what became known as the "big ship" project in 1946. The U.S. government was to build and pay for most of her, while United States Lines would own (under lease) and operate her. Early estimates were that she would be about 48,000 tons and cost almost $70 million—over a billion dollars in today's money. Despite the high cost, enthusiasm spread: there was further, albeit brief thinking of a companion ship of 40,000 tons. While she too would be capable of high speeds, it was soon determined that passenger comfort might be at risk in a vessel of such smaller proportions. Only the "big ship"—eventually named the *United States*—endured. [Built by Newport News Shipbuilding & Drydock Company, Newport News, Virginia, 1952. 53,329 gross tons; 990 feet long; 101 feet wide. Steam turbines, quadruple screw. Service speed 33 knots. 1,928 passengers (871 first class, 508 cabin class, 549 tourist class).]

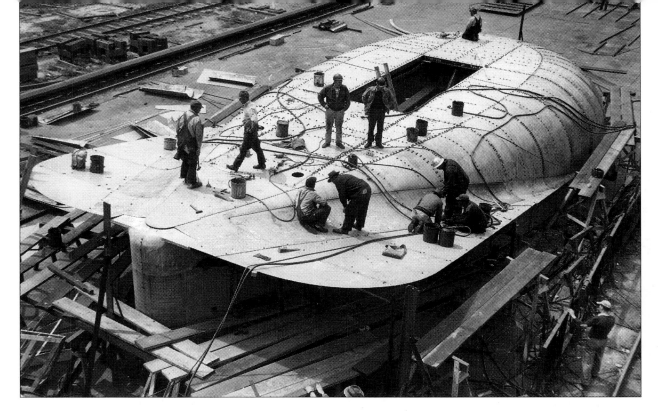

The *United States* was 70 percent complete when she was first floated. Aside from completing the physical structures of the ship, there was the mind-boggling process of procuring all the items needed on board: for example, 125,000 pieces of chinaware, 6,000 crystal goblets, 7,000 bedspreads, 4,000 passenger blankets, 44,000 bed sheets, 81,000 face towels, 44,000 pillow slips, and seven caskets for the ship's hospital. For the overall design 8,000 drawings were made along with 1,200,000 blueprints. The speed trials for what was then said to be the world's fastest liner were set for May and June of 1952. In every way they were a blazing success. She looked magnificent cutting through the water *(bottom)*. The *United States* was indeed a symbol of the best in American design, construction, and technology. She was well ahead of every other pas-senger ship then afloat. On the trials in early June 1,700 guests and reporters and two-thirds of her intended crew were aboard for runs off the Virginia coast. There were crash stops, full rudder tests, stability tests, even a stint in full reverse at 20 knots! The absolute top speed seemed to be a secret, but at least a few guests were told that it was an astonishing 39.38 knots. This represented an extraordinary total shaft output of nearly 242,000 horsepower, compared to the 158,000 maximum of the *Queen Mary*, then the world's fastest liner. Surely, the *United States* would be the Atlantic speed champion. It was later revealed that during these trials the 990-foot long liner actually made an incredible 43 knots for a short time and even outpaced an escorting Navy destroyer.

The *United States* received one of New York harbor's greatest and warmest receptions when she arrived on June 23, 1952 *(above)*. She had come on an overnight trip from Newport News with 1,200 invited guests aboard, including no less than 167 reporters. Dozens of tugs and other harbor boats escorted her to Pier 86, where she remained for over a week of receptions, dinners, luncheons, and guided tours. Instantly, she was the most publicized ship in the world.

The greatest test for the *United States* was her maiden voyage to Europe. She left Pier 86 *(opposite, top)* at noon on July 3, bound for Southampton and Le Havre. Carrying 1,700 passengers (including Margaret Truman, representing her father, President Harry Truman), she easily beat the *Queen Mary's* record. On July 7 she officially captured the Blue Ribbon with a record run to the English coast of 3 days, 10 hours, and 40 minutes, at an average speed of 35.59 knots. This was 3.9 knots faster than the *Mary's* record from 1938. On the returning westbound crossing, when she

averaged 34.51 knots, she reentered New York harbor flying the forty-foot-long Blue Ribbon banner. Her welcome included 400 different whistle salutes and a ticker tape parade for her crew along lower Broadway. There were immediate rumors of even higher speed and greater records, but in fact there was no need or reason for the added expense. The ship became enormously popular. Within her first year she was continuously booked at over 90 percent occupancy.

There was a pleasing simplicity about the interior decor of the new superliner. For example, her first-class dining room *(opposite, bottom)* used only a minimum of artwork for enhancement. Perhaps one of the best-known stories about the *United States* involved her extremely high fire safety standards. There was, it was often said, absolutely no wood on board except in the butcher's block and the piano. (Steinway & Sons, despite urgings from William Francis Gibbs, refused to make an aluminum piano.)

The decorators of the *United States* often opted for the functional. The ship was not overtly luxurious or even cozy, but impeccably maintained and always comfortable. While she had a loyal following and remained very popular almost until the end of her days, she lacked the grandeur and the glitter of, say, the French Line passenger ships or the wood-paneled charm of the Cunard and Holland-America liners. The *United States* set the tone, in fact, for almost all other subsequent American passenger ships of the 1950s. Her first-class main lounge *(right)* was especially popular.

The Navajo Cocktail Lounge *(left)*, also in first class, was furnished with vinyl-covered chairs that were typical of the *United States*.

The sitting room *(right)* of interconnecting suite U 87-89-91, the so-called Duck Suite (with a bedroom beyond and another not shown), was the finest quarters aboard the *United States*. In her maiden season this space was priced at $930 per person for a five-day crossing. Minimum passage rates started at $360 in first class, $230 in cabin class, and $170 in tourist class.

At the end of each year, usually in December, the *United States* returned to the Newport News shipyard in Virginia for her annual overhaul. In the course of three to four weeks she was cleaned and painted, and her bottom was scraped and her sea chests (side openings for water release) cleaned. The propellers were changed, and the bow section was reinforced. Work crews, like those in this nighttime view dated December 1953 *(above)*, continued around the clock so that the liner would be ready on time, usually for a mid-January eastbound crossing.

The *United States* was rarely delayed by weather. Even with heavy ice accumulation in the north slip of Pier 86, February 18, 1958 *(above)*, she berthed only thirty minutes later than planned. The greatest worry, especially in later years, was strikes by American seamen. These often kept the liner idle for weeks if not months at a time, thus interrupting her schedules as well as the plans of passengers. Profits were often diminished by these strikes.

The *United States* was often included in the great gatherings of some of the world's largest and grandest liners along New York City's "Luxury Liner Row." In this aerial view *(opposite, top)*, dated May 28, 1958, five Atlantic liners are in port together: (from top to bottom) the *Vulcania*, Italian Line; the *America* and then the *United States*; the *Flandre*, French Line; and, just docking, the *Queen Elizabeth*, Cunard Line, then the world's largest liner.

Celebrities of the 1950s and '60s were often passengers on the world's fastest liner. There was former President Eisenhower and Queen Frederika of Greece, Emperor Haile Selassie of Ethiopia and President Tubman of Liberia, Eleanor Roosevelt and Irving

Berlin, Cary Grant and John Wayne, Greta Garbo and Marilyn Monroe, Leopold Stokowski and Leonard Bernstein. But by far the most publicized passengers to board the *United States* were the Duke and Duchess of Windsor *(opposite, bottom left)*, who crossed twice a year in the ship between 1952 and 1969. Traveling with their own servants as well as their dogs, the former king and his American wife brought their own crested china and even bed linens. They often departed with as many as ninety-five pieces of luggage, including many big Vuitton trunks. On all but one occasion they came and went at Le Havre, which was convenient to their home in Paris. But in this photo from September 1967 they are being greeted by reporters at Southampton. They had returned to England for the celebration of a special centenary: the birth of Queen Mary, the duke's mother. They would be guests of the duke's niece, Queen Elizabeth II.

Another *United States* passenger was artist Salvador Dali *(opposite, bottom right)*, posing for the press and a group of Girl Scouts prior to departing from New York in 1963. He often traveled with his pet ocelot.

In the face of mounting losses throughout the 1960s the *United States* was decommissioned in November 1969. She was laid up at a Norfolk, Virginia, pier *(above)*, her home for the next twenty-three years. Amidst talk that she would be reactivated as a passenger or cruise ship, there were also reports that the U.S. Navy wanted her as a hospital and then a barracks ship, that other interests planned to use her as an industrial exhibit ship, as a moored hotel, or even as a floating missionary center. She was, in fact, sold to Seattle-based businessman Richard Hadley in 1980. He planned to refit her for cruis-

ing: to Hawaii, the Caribbean, even occasional nostalgic Atlantic crossings. In deepening decay, she was briefly drydocked, as shown here on May 5, 1980, just prior to the official transfer to Hadley. But little else occurred. A conversion for further service in the early 1980s was reported to cost $200 million, or over three times her original construction cost forty years before. The *United States* at anchor was neglected further. Her lounges turned musty, her hull was streaked in rust, and layers of dead harbor birds began to fill the once pristine indoor promenades. In 1984 many of her fittings and furnishings were auctioned off, realizing $5 million.

In deep debt and running from creditors, the *United States* was herself auctioned off to Turkish interests called Marmara Marine in February 1992. That summer she was towed to Turkey, to the small port of Tuzla Gölü, supposedly to await rebuilding. There were rumors that she might be operated by the Cunard Line and run in tandem with their *Queen Elizabeth 2*. But funding never came, and the Turks soon lost interest. In the summer of 1996 she was towed back to American waters, arriving at Philadelphia with interiors stripped and empty *(left)*. As the idea of reviving the old passenger ship seemed less and less likely, one strong rumor (in 1998) was that she would become a floating hotel and mini-convention center moored along New York's West Side at 39th Street. Other rumors were that she would become an army barracks in Kuwait or a museum, or that she might be sold to shipbreakers in Texas. At the time of writing, however, no project has materialized. Thus far the ship has been idle for more than thirty years.

MONTEREY (1952). Three of the *Mariner*-class freighters created during the Korean War were soon rebuilt as passenger ships. The Matson Line, wanting to revive its South Pacific service, took two of these cargo vessels—the *Free State Mariner* and the *Pine Tree Mariner*—and converted them as the *Monterey (above)* and *Mariposa* in 1956. The decor aboard both had a Pacific-Polynesian theme, muted by the overall simplistic tone common to American passenger ships of the period. [Built by Bethlehem Steel Corporation, Sparrows Point, Maryland, 1952. 14,799 gross tons; 563 feet long; 76 feet wide. Steam turbines, single screw. Service speed 20 knots. 365 all-first-class passengers.]

MARIPOSA (1953). The *Mariposa*, on her maiden voyage in October 1956 *(below)*, and her sister ran on forty-two-day itineraries from San Francisco and Los Angeles down to the South Seas. Their passenger accommodations were arranged on five decks, and amenities included air conditioning, stabilizers, outdoor pool, movie theater, beauty salon, and barber shop. There were two lanai suites and six deluxe cabins, all with sitting area, bedroom, and bath. The other cabins had private baths as well. Public rooms included the Pool Terrace, Outrigger Bar, Polynesian Club, and Southern Cross Lounge. Matson Lines left the U.S. passenger ship business in 1970, and for the next eight years both the *Mariposa* and the *Monterey* sailed for another San Francisco-based operator, the Pacific Far East Line, (PFEL). The *Mariposa* was subsequently sold, then reactivated in 1983 as the Chinese-owned *Jin Jiang*. She later became the *Queen of Jing Jiang* and then *Heng Li* before being scrapped in 1996. The *Monterey* was sold to the newly formed Aloha Pacific Cruises, a short-lived U.S.-flag operation, in 1986. Expecting to capitalize on her original name, the new owners sent her on inter-Hawaiian Island cruises. But the time was not right and in 1990 she was sold to Italian shipowners, who still sail her as the *Monterey* but under the Panamanian flag. [Built by Bethlehem Steel Corporation, Quincy, Massachusetts, 1953. 14,812 gross tons; 563 feet long; 76 feet wide. Steam turbines, single screw. Service speed 20 knots. 365 all-first-class passengers.]

ATLANTIC. Another *Mariner*-class freighter conversion was that of the *Badger Mariner*. She followed the rebuilding of Matson's all-first-class *Mariposa* and *Monterey*, and became the two-class, transatlantic-style *Atlantic* of 1958. She is seen moving under the Brooklyn Bridge *(opposite, top)*. She had far larger passenger accommodations and was aimed at the economy, tourist class trade, which was soon to decline considerably in the face of airline competition. While a comfortable vessel, the *Atlantic* was too late to be a success. For her owners, the American Banner Line, a joint venture between the Bernstein shipping interests and the Seafarers' International Union, she lasted but two seasons before being sold to the American Export Lines in December 1959. [Built by Sun Shipbuilding & Dry Dock Company, Chester, Pennsylvania, 1953. 14,138 gross tons; 564 feet long; 76 feet wide. Steam turbines, single screw. Service speed 20 knots. 880 passengers (40 first class, 840 tourist class).]

American Export Lines had long wanted a third ship for their New York–Mediterranean service (joining the far larger *Independence* and *Constitution*). To sail the Atlantic as well as on off-season cruises to the Caribbean, the *Atlantic* was repainted all white *(opposite, bottom)* and was active for them from 1960 until 1967. Her fate was uncertain for several years before, in 1971, she was sold to the C. Y. Tung Shipping Group. She became the "semes-

ter at sea" university cruise ship *Universe Campus* (a name shortened to *Universe* in 1976) and was later used on summertime cruises to Alaska out of Vancouver. She was refitted in 1994 for extended service, but shortly thereafter her aged boilers gave out. In April 1996 she was handed over to shipbreakers at Alang, India.

SANTA ROSA (1958). The Grace Line were masters of the art of public relations in the 1950s and 1960s. For one promotion they brought a llama from Peru to their New York sales office on Fifth Avenue. In introducing their new *Santa Rosa* and *Santa Paula*, Grace wanted to differentiate them from their 1932-built namesakes, which they were to replace. On August 28, 1957, the twenty-five-year-old *Santa Rosa*, northbound from the Caribbean to New York, made a special detour to the James River in Virginia. Just off the Newport News shipyard, she was specially dressed in flags and slowed as her replacement was launched and moved to a fitting-out berth at the yard *(above)*. Indeed, it was a unique occasion, the first of its kind in passenger ship history. The new *Rosa* was delivered in June 1958, while the older ship was laid up (along with her sister, the *Santa Paula*) before being sold to Greek buyers in 1960. [Built by Newport News Shipbuilding & Drydock Company, Newport News, Virginia, 1958. 15,371 gross tons; 584 feet long; 84 feet wide. Steam turbines, twin screw. Service speed 20 knots. 300 all-first-class passengers.]

SANTA PAULA (1958). The new *Santa Paula (top)*, added in September 1958, and her sistership ran Grace Line's weekly thirteen-day Caribbean service, sailing from New York to Curaçao, La Guaira, Aruba, Kingston, Port-au-Prince, and Port Everglades (Florida). Minimum round-trip rates began at $595, then the highest fares of their kind. The *Santa Paula* and her sister relied on cruise passengers as well as one-way traffic (there was still a business and family trade, particularly between New York and La Guaira). The ships' accommodations included more suites and deluxe staterooms than ordinary cabins. Both ships had advanced fire safety systems as well as sophisticated cargo-handling gear, which included the novelty of folding hatch covers. When the *Santa Paula* was first introduced she made an all-day, 125-mile trip up the Hudson River from New York Harbor to Albany. She was the largest ship of her kind to make such a voyage. [Built by Newport News Shipbuilding & Drydock Company, Newport News, Virginia, 1958. 15,371 gross tons; 584 feet long; 84 feet wide. Steam turbines, twin screw. Service speed 20 knots. 300 all-first-class passengers.]

The Grace Line, which became the Prudential-Grace Lines through a merger in 1970, decided to decommission both the *Santa Rosa* and the *Santa Paula*. The *Rosa* was subsequently laid up in the backwaters of Baltimore harbor before being sold in 1989 to Greek interests, Regency Cruises, who had her rebuilt as the greatly enlarged, 960-capacity *Regent Rainbow (bottom)*. When Regency collapsed in the fall of 1995, she was again laid up for a time before being auctioned off to Cypriot owners, the Louis Cruise Lines. As the renamed *Emerald*, she currently sails under charter to the London-based Thomson Air-Sea Cruises. She has made Mediterranean as well as Caribbean cruises. The *Santa Paula* was sold in 1972 to the Sun Line. They brought her to Greece, intending to rebuild her as the Aegean cruise ship *Stella Polaris*, but these plans were abandoned following the great fuel oil increases of 1973–74. She was refitted, from 1976 to 1980, brought to Kuwait, and installed as a permanently moored floating hotel, first called Kuwait Marriott Hotel and then Ramada Al Salaam Hotel. She was, however, bombed and set afire during the Gulf War in February 1991.

ARGENTINA. In the same year that the Grace Line introduced the new sisterships, Moore-McCormack Lines added a set of brand-new twins for the run from New York to the east coast of South America. Named *Brasil* (introduced in September 1958 and using the Portuguese spelling at the request of the Brazilian government) and *Argentina* (added that December), they were among the most expensive ships of their day, costing $25 million each. Unique in being the largest passenger liners yet built in the American South, they were designed with luxurious accommodations as well as considerable cargo space for thirty-one-day round-trip voyages between New York and Barbados or Trinidad, Rio de Janeiro, Santos, Montevideo, and turnaround at Buenos Aires. They too were intended to rely on both round-trip cruise passengers (minimum fare was $1,110 in 1959) as well as the one-way trade. Sailing on Friday evenings, Moore-McCormack advertised that Rio was ten "working days" away, with an arrival early on Monday morning. But these ships were less than successful and

were withdrawn by September 1969. Eventually they were sold off to a string of foreign owners, beginning with the Holland America Line.

The *Argentina* became the *Veendam* and then the *Monarch Star, Brasil* (for a brief charter in 1974–75), back to *Monarch Star*, then *Bermuda Star, Enchanted Isle, Commodore Hotel*, and finally *Enchanted Isle*. The *Brasil* changed to *Volendam* and then *Monarch Sun*, followed by *Island Sun, Liberte, Canada Star, Queen of Bermuda, Enchanted Seas*, and in 1996 *Universe Explorer*. In this 1987 photo (**above**) the two liners sail past New York City's World Trade Center towers: the *Bermuda Star* is in front of the *Canada Star*. Both ships remain in service to date, as the *Enchanted Isle* (ex-*Argentina*) and *Universe Explorer* (ex-*Brasil*). [Built by Ingalls Shipbuilding Corporation, Pascagoula, Mississippi, 1958. 23,500 gross tons; 617 feet long; 86 feet wide. Steam turbines, twin screw. Service speed 23 knots. 553 all-first-class passengers.]

SAVANNAH. In the mid-1950s the U.S. government, namely the Maritime Administration, saw a bright future in nuclear-powered ships. The prototype was a $60 million passenger-cargo vessel, first called *Atom Queen*, but named *Savannah* in honor of the first steamship to cross the Atlantic some 140 years before, in 1819. Painted all-white, sleek in every way, and with a marquis-shaped housing in place of an actual funnel, she was designed with luxurious quarters for sixty passengers. Laid down in May 1958, launched in July 1959, and completed in December 1961, she received great publicity before her actual maiden voyage in August 1962. At first managed by the New York-based States Marine Lines, a freighter company, she eventually passed to American Export Lines (renamed American Export-Isbrandtsen Lines in 1962). On her maiden call at Barcelona, Spain, the *Savannah* encountered the *Independence*, seen in the background of this 1962 photo *(above)*. Back in the United States she was sometimes sent off on unusual voyages—one took her overnight from New York to Bridgeport, Conn., with passengers paying $15 each. But the *Savannah* soon proved to be a problem. She required specially trained crews and increased security at her ports of call, even being denied entry to some places. She was often docked stern-first as a precaution against a possible fuel leak. Each refueling cost $268,000. Consequently, there were no successors, and the U.S. government soon lost interest in nuclear-powered commercial ships. By the end of 1971 American Export had lost interest as well. First laid up at Savannah, Georgia, the ship was moved in 1981 to Charleston, South Carolina, and used as a museum. A subsequent victim of financial as well as maintenance problems, she was returned to Maritime Administration care and, in 1994, moved to the reserve fleet in the James River, Virginia. [Built by New York Shipbuilding Corporation, Camden, New Jersey, 1958–62. 13,599 gross tons; 595 feet long; 78 feet wide. Nuclear reactor plus steam turbines, twin screw. Service speed 20 knots. 60 all-first-class passengers.]

AMERICAN CRUISING. While U.S.-flag passenger ships all but disappeared after the 1970s, the country now supports the greatest cruise trade anywhere. Two Florida ports, Miami and Port Everglades, and San Juan, Puerto Rico, are the world's busiest cruise departure ports. At Miami's Dodge Island terminals *(opposite, top)*, five of the world's most popular cruise ships, all of them foreign-flag, gathered on March 9, 1996. The 70,200-ton *Inspiration* has just arrived on her maiden voyage. Immediately behind are two other members of the giant Carnival Cruise Lines' fleet, the *Celebration* (left) and the *Imagination*. Beyond is the Norwegian Cruise Lines' *Norway* and then Royal Caribbean International's *Sovereign of the Seas*.

All in all, U.S.-flag passenger ships are enjoying a major revival. In early 1999, New Orleans–headquartered American Classic Voyages announced plans for two 71,000-tonners for their American Hawaii Cruises division. Orders were signed that spring with the Ingalls Shipbuilding Corporation at Pascagoula, Mississippi for these 1,900-capacity ships. Costing over $400 million each, they are the largest American-flag liners ever. In addition, the company planned for at least five 226-passenger coastal cruise ships for a new subsidiary, Delta Queen Coastal Cruises, that would offer vacation voyages from the likes of Halifax, Boston, New York, Norfolk, Jacksonville, Miami, San Francisco, Seattle, Juneau, and Anchorage. Easily the most ambitious plan, although still in the planning stages, was that of the *Westin World City* *(opposite, bottom)*. With three towers rising on a long hull, she would be American-built and the largest passenger vessel yet, at 250,000 tons and 1,246 feet in length. She would carry approximately 6,000 passengers and have 2,000 crew members. Her construction costs were said to be near $2 billion by 1999. Said to be a "resort within herself," she would have massive portals in the stern section that would open to reveal a large, self-contained marina. Four "day cruisers," each with a capacity of 400, would dock inside the ship and shuttle passengers within a fifty-mile radius. Other facilities would include a deck designated as a re-creation of "Main Street USA," art galleries, museums, tropical gardens, a sports arena, sidewalk cafes and nightclubs, a 2,500-seat theater, several pools, a 100,000-book library, a 1,500-seat conference center, a stock brokerage office, an arts complex, a dozen or so restaurants, and a complete shopping center. These plans suggest a busy future for the U.S. cruise industry, opening a new chapter in American passenger ship history.

Bibliography

Billings, Henry. *Superliner SS United States*. New York: Viking Press, 1954.

Bonsor, N. R. P. *North Atlantic Seaway*. Prescot, Lancashire: T. Stephenson & Sons Ltd., 1955.

Braynard, Frank O. *By Their Works Ye Shall Know Them*. New York: Gibbs & Cox, 1968.

————. *Lives of the Liners*. New York: Cornell Maritime Press, 1947.

———— and Miller, William H. *Fifty Famous Liners*, Vols. 1–3. Cambridge, England: Patrick Stephens Ltd., 1982–86.

Cooke, Anthony. *Emigrant Ships*. London: Carmania Press Ltd., 1992.

Crowdy, Michael (ed.). *Marine News*. Kendal, Cumbria: World Ship Society, 1964–69.

Devol, George (ed.). *Ocean & Cruise News*. Stamford, Conn.: World Ocean & Cruise Society, 1980–99.

Dunn, Laurence. *Passenger Liners*. Southampton, England: Adlard Coles Ltd., 1961, 1965 (rev. ed.).

Eisele, Peter (ed.). *Steamboat Bill*. New York: Steamship Historical Society, 1966–99.

Emmons, Frederick. *American Passenger Ships*. Newark, Del.: University of Delaware Press, 1985.

Goldberg, Mark H. *Caviar & Cargo*. Kings Point, N.Y.: American Merchant Marine Museum, 1992.

————. *Going Bananas*. Kings Point, N.Y.: American Merchant Marine Museum, 1993.

Kludas, Arnold. *Die Grossen Passagier-Schiffe der Welt*. Hamburg: Koehlers Verlagsgesellschaft mbH, 1997.

————. *Great American Passenger Ships of the World*, Vols. 1–5. Cambridge, England: Patrick Stephens Ltd., 1972–76.

————. *Great Passenger Ships of the World*. Vol. 6. Cambridge, England: Patrick Stephens Ltd., 1986.

Kludas, Arnold. *Great Passenger Ships of the World Today*. Sparkford, England: Patrick Stephens Ltd., 1992.

Miller, William H. *The Last Atlantic Liners*. London: Conway Maritime Press Ltd., 1985.

————. *SS United States: The History of American's Greatest Liner*. Sparkford, England, 1991.

————. *Passenger Liners American Style*. London: Carmania Press, Ltd., 1999.

Plowman, Peter. *Emigrant Ships to Luxury Liners*. Kensington, Australia: New South Wales University Press, 1992.

Sawyer, L. A., and Mitchell, W. H. *From America to the United States*, Vols. 1–4. Kendal, Cumbria: World Ship Society, 1979–1986.

Ships Monthly (1982–1999). Burton-on-Trent, Staffordshire: Waterway Productions Ltd.

Towline (1950–1996). New York: Moran Towing & Transportation Co.

Watson, Milton. *US Passenger Liners Since 1945*. Wellingborough, Northamptonshire: Patrick Stephens Ltd., 1988.

Index of Ships in Illustrations

The different names the ships covered in this book have had during their careers at sea are generally mentioned in the text. Where relevant, these names are carried in alphabetical order in the following list.

Acadia, 32–33
Acropolis, 51
African Endeavor, 71–72
African Enterprise, 71–72
African Planet, 78
Alaska, 40
Alcoa Cavalier, 76
Alcoa Corsair, 79
Alcoa Cruiser, 79
Aleutian, 40
Algonquin, 32–33
Alsatia, 66
America (1905), 11, 12
America (1939), 61–68
America, 106–107
American Farmer, 21
American Importer, 26–27
American Legion, 18–19
American Shipper, 26–27
American Star, 68
American Trader, 18–19
Amerika, 11, 12
Amerika, 46–47
Ancon, 70–71
Argentina, 113
Arosa Star, 36
Athinai, 51
Atlantic, 111
Atlantic, 25
Australis, 66

Bahama Star, 36
Barnett, 26
Barrett, 88
Bay State, 18
Belgenland, 15
Belgic, 15
Berkshire, 36–37
Bermuda Star, 113
Blanche F. Sigman, 80–81
Borinquen, 36
Brabantia. 13
Brasil (1958), 113
Brazil, 31

Cabo de Hornos, 20–21
California, 28

Canada Star, 113
Cavalier, 76
Celebration, 114
City of Hamburg, 22
City of Honolulu, 14
City of San Francisco, 22
Colombia, 34–35
Columbia, 15
Constitution, 92–93, 95, 97–98
Conte Biancamano, 80–81
Cristóbal, 70
Cristoforo Colombo, 66

David C. Shanks, 79
Del Mar, 74
Delbrasil, 71
Dixie, 36–37

Eclipse, 22
Edmund B. Alexander, 46–47
Ellinis, 59
Emerald, 112
Empire State, 21
Empire State, 88
Europa, 98
Evangeline, 34–35
Excalibur, 48
Excalibur, 75
Exochorda, 48–49
Exochorda, 76

Finland, 15
Flandre, 106–107
Florida, 38–39

Geiger, 88
Gen. Alexander M. Patch, 86
Gen. D. E. Aultman, 87
Gen. Hugh J. Gaffey, 85
Gen. J. C. Breckinridge, 84
Gen. Maurice Rose, 86
Gen. Simon B. Buckner, 86
Gen. Ulysses S. Grant, 14
Gen. W. M. Black, 87
Gen. William O. Darby, 86
Gen. William Weigel, 85
George Clymer, 78

George F. Elliott, 71
George Washington, 10–11, 12
Great Northern, 39

H.F. Alexander, 39
Henry Lee, 48–49
Hermitage, 80–81
Homeric, 59

Imagination, 114
Independence, 93–99
Inspiration, 114
Iroquois, 32
Italia, 80–81

J. A. Mowinckel, 18–19
John Ericsson, 80–81
Joseph Hewes, 48
Joseph T. Dickman, 17

Kaiser Wilhelm II, 12
Kiautschou, 14
Koda, 18
Kronprinzessin Cecilie, 9, 12
Kroonland, 15
Kungsholm, 80–81

Leviathan, 1–7
Limburgia, 13
Lombardia, 13
Lone Star State, 17
Lurline, 55, 57–59

Madawaska, 14
Malolo, 24–25
Malolo, 57
Manhattan, 42–43
Manhattan, 45–47
Marianna VI, 73
Marigold, 20–21
Mariposa, 109
Mariposa, 55
Matsonia, 25
Matsonia, 59
Maua, 22
Mauretania, 66
Mazatlán, 40

Mexico, 40
Monterey, 109
Monterey, 56–57, 59
Monticello, 12
Morro Castle, 52–53
Mount Vernon, 45
Mount Vernon, 9, 12

New Bahama Star, 39
Norway, 114

Oceanic Independence, 98–99
Old North State, 21
Oriente, 54

Peninsular State, 17
Pennsylvania, 26–27
Portland, 87
President Adams, 88
President Cleveland, 90–91
President Coolidge, 54–55
President Harding, 17
President Jackson, 18–19
President Jackson, 88
President Madison, 18
President Pierce, 17
President Polk, 73
President Quezon, 18
President Roosevelt, 17, 18–19
President Roosevelt, 26–27

President Taft, 17
President Van Buren, 21
President Wilson, 21
President Wilson, 90–91
Princess Matoika, 14
Puerto Rico, 36
Pvt. Elden H. Johnson, 79
Pvt. William H. Thomas, 79

Queen Elizabeth, 106–107
Queen Elizabeth, 66
Queen Frederica, 25
Queen Mary, 82

Regent Rainbow, 112
Reliance, 13
Republic, 13
Resolute, 13

Santa Elena, 48–49
Santa Isabel, 74
Santa Lucia, 48–49
Santa Maria, 26
Santa Paula (1958), 112
Santa Paula, 48–51
Santa Rosa (1958), 111
Santa Rosa, 48–50
Savannah, 114
Scanyork, 22
Schenectady, 22

Sovereign of the Seas, 114
Stanford White, 80–81
Stevens, 76
Surriento, 26

Takasago Maru, 83
Tarsus, 48–49
Thomas H. Barry, 54

U. S. Grant, 14
United States, 66
United States, 98, 100–108
Uruguay, 28–29

Vaterland, 2
Veragua, 51
Ville de Bruges, 17
Ville de Liege, 21
Virginia, 26–27
Vulcania, 106–107

Wakefield, 45
Washington, 26–27
Washington, 44–47
West Point, 64
Westin World City, 114
William P. Biddle, 22

Zeilin, 18–19